PLAY THE SYSTEM

PLAY THE
SYSTEM

A Corporate Rebel's Guide to Make
Your Organization LISTEN and CHANGE

NORA GANESCU

NEW YORK

LONDON • NASHVILLE • MELBOURNE • VANCOUVER

PLAY THE SYSTEM
A Corporate Rebel's Guide to Make Your
Organization LISTEN and CHANGE

© 2020 **NORA GANESCU**

Published in New York, New York, by Morgan James Publishing in partnership with Difference Press. Morgan James is a trademark of Morgan James, LLC.
www.MorganJamesPublishing.com

ISBN 978-1-64279-558-5 paperback
ISBN 978-1-64279-559-2 eBook
Library of Congress Control Number: 2019938316

Cover Design by:
Rachel Lopez
www.r2cdesign.com

Interior Design by:
Bonnie Bushman
The Whole Caboodle Graphic Design

Morgan James is a proud partner of Habitat for Humanity Peninsula
and Greater Williamsburg. Partners in building since 2006.

Get involved today! Visit
www.MorganJamesBuilds.com

To my mother Agnes, my rock, my teacher,
and my unending source of love with
gratitude for my roots and my wings

Table of Contents

The Life-Draining "System"

"Never doubt that a small group of thoughtful, committed citizens can change the world; indeed, it's the only thing that ever has."

– Margaret Mead

I am looking at you, reader. As if through the reverse looking glass, I feel that through the pages of this book not only will you get to meet me, but I also get a glimpse of you.

The fact that you picked up this book tells me that you could have lots in common (when it comes to working in your organization) with some of my favorite people: my clients.

1

My coaching clients are people like you who bring great talent, cool ideas, and insights to the table (and they are great fun, too). Above all, they care. It matters to them, as I am sure it matters to you, what kind of organizations they are working for and how those organizations function. They want to take pride in their workplace, and they want to be able to give their best to their colleagues and the people they serve through their work. They are engaged.

Often, they have great ideas for change and innovation: how to make the organization better for the employees, how to eliminate waste (not only materials, but people's energy and time), and how to serve their clients better. They know how to achieve the goals of the organization better, and care about its mission.

They find meaning in their work and they want to make a difference in the world (and their immediate environment).

Is this you? Do I see you clearly? (And don't think that my description is so general that it is true for everybody. All the statistics show that over seventy percent of the employees worldwide are disengaged. You are not one of them!)

Now here's an interesting aspect: many companies treat engagement of their employees like some elusive Holy Grail that is very hard to achieve and has to be measured and managed. But here you are, somebody who is engaged and committed. So how come that what you experience on an everyday basis is draining the life and excitement out of you?

Instead of feeling that your engagement is valued, you feel that you'd be better off if you didn't care. Your ideas are not supported or even heard. You receive little to no support from your direct management for trying out anything new or innovative—sometimes not even for something that would be common sense. And it's not just the hierarchy; there seems to be also very little appetite among your peers to press for changes. Yes, there is a lot of talk and complaining in the corridors, but real action, a new approach to innovation, let alone some fundamental change? Not so much.

Most people would like to see changes for the better, big and small, but only if somebody else does them. So here you are with all that you could do and create, trapped in what feels like a very hostile environment.

Sometimes it is your direct boss or their boss who is the biggest block.

This was the case for Diana, one of my clients. Diana is an accomplished leader in her own right. She has studied in multiple countries and has masters degrees in Hindi and human rights education and has worked for charities around the world, in leadership positions. At forty, the mother of two sons and the main breadwinner in her family, she has achieved one of her long-held dreams: to work for an international organization known for its values, might, and good work in the world.

She was leading a regional office of this organization with a team of ten people, and while she accomplished one successful project after the other, she also got more and more burned out and discouraged. Her innovative projects were invariably met with roadblocks and skepticism by her management. Everything felt like an uphill battle. When she was advocating for better work conditions for her staff, asking that the organization live up to its stated values and standards, she was informed by well-meaning colleagues from the headquarters that she cannot expect such a thing. She was not to expect, for example, that all the provisions of the staff regulation would apply to all employees. Also, she really should not expect any meaningful change too soon (like this decade). This was (apparently) not how it works.

She found herself ever more exhausted and on a collision course between her need to stand up for her values, contribute her best and most innovative work, and the leaders who would politely dismiss her and an organization and culture that seemed to be outdated and unmovable.

She felt reduced to a cog in a soulless machine, built to perform functions accurately but ultimately stripped of her creativity, challenged by the compromise of her values and integrity. She was also exhausted and burned out by trying so hard to get through walls of rejection and interference. From the perspective of an outsider, Diana was successful and accomplished. But from her perspective, she was losing more and more of herself every day.

This is not a rare story. Actually, this is one of the most common stories that I encounter in any company or organization. But why? All companies that employ people depend on them to show up with engagement and commitment, to seek to improve when they see an opportunity. So why is it that so, so many of them seemingly cannot deal at all with real engagement, vision, creativity, and innovation? There are many, many reasons. And here are some of the most important.

- **The companies are not designed for that.** Most of the organizations in our times are modeled on machines (based on a paradigm from the 19th century). Following this perspective, people are regarded as "components," with a very narrow scope and very specific function. They are expected to perform that function to perfection, sometimes under great pressure, but nothing more. A creative component that has ideas and wants to significantly impact the functioning of the machine is considered a malfunction that has to be repaired. No part should have initiatives. Of course, this is a metaphor and the reality is not so extreme. But it is a metaphor that has shaped our thinking about organizations for over a century and a half and its impact cannot be denied.

- **We are invested in the status quo.** Most people have accepted the dominant metaphor and have invested themselves in creating this reality. This is especially true for many people in high leadership positions. They have studied management. They learned how to make the machine work more efficiently and this system has worked for them: and they are rewarded with symbols of appreciation and greater degrees of freedom.

- **The senior managers see their liberty and appreciation as badges of achievement that can be**

granted to the few deserving ones but not to all.
Similarly, even if counterintuitively, many people from
the lower ranks of the hierarchy support this view. They
trade freedom for the burden of taking responsibility
for decisions and caring too much about work. There
is a funny comfort in complaining but not having to
do anything about it. And most people from all levels
are scared of changes and will prefer to sustain the
status quo over the significant disruption that would
be unleashed if anybody would freely bring their best
gifts and creativity to work every day.

- **Simply put: it's bad management.** Good managers are
actually rare and hard to find. A Gallup study found
that eight in ten managers fail at their job of creating
an environment that affirms what is best in everybody.
Instead, people are surviving in hostile environments
devoid of appreciation and support, trying hard to at
least deliver what is expected of them in these harsh
conditions. Engagement is taken for granted. But
a real commitment to the values of the company or
to the greater good is too challenging (especially if it
stands in contradiction with their personal wellbeing).
Often managers are acting this way out of lack of skill
and insecurity, so dealing with innovative ideas feels
threatening and difficult for them.

So where does this leave you? Shall you abandon all hope
here? Shall you stop bringing new ideas, stop trying to realize
that project you care about deeply at work? Of course not!

You have more resources than you think. Some of them are in you: your skills, talent, and energy. Many of them are around you and might as yet be invisible to you: the richness of ideas, the can-do spirit, the creative genius of collective intelligence, and the concrete possibilities that you will learn to galvanize around your own sense of purpose. You have an important role to play, an amazing contribution to make, and your energy and creativity would be a terrible thing to waste. But on your journey to be successful, you have to unlock some treasures, resources, and superpowers (just like in a computer game). I assembled in this book the map and the keys to these treasures, so your adventure becomes easier and more fun.

You will find very specific steps that you can take, methods and tools that you can use, and challenges designed to open new perspectives and possibilities for you.

And will you succeed? As Dr. Seuss says, "Yes! You will indeed! 99 and 3/4 percent guaranteed!"

Chapter 2

My Story

I feel so passionately about this because I have been there—repeatedly. I was always somebody who was the opposite of cool and distanced, but rather suffering from a case of too much enthusiasm, always looking for using all that I've got, doing the best job I can, and searching for meaning in what I do. Maybe you can relate.

So it is almost by design that every time I was working in an organization, I would come in on a high, wanting to change the world, and then start to bump against barriers very soon. It seems like part of my induction to any job was a comprehensive tour of all that I cannot do. Not possible, not a priority, no money, no time, the hierarchy doesn't care. When asking about the reasoning for some of the work that kept people around me stressed, I heard things like, "We know that this doesn't really make sense, but headquarters wants it this way," "We need to cover our backs," "It is somebody's ego project, but nobody believes in it," "It's always been done like this, and we cannot change it," and so on.

In my quest to contribute and make a meaningful contribution to my work, I would start to hit the walls really fast. As time passed, I happily became more skillful at navigating those situations and realized some projects dear to my heart. This is also why, when I work with coaching clients from organizations as part of my portfolio of coaching managers and other people who want to make a difference, I feel recognition and instant kinship with the amazing people that come to me.

The feeling that I was reduced to a cog in a machine, that I could do better but I was kept back by "rules" and conventions that (at a closer look) did not make sense to me, or being discounted and overruled by big egos (with lots of power in the hierarchy) was hard to take.

This is my rebellious streak, maybe coming from my childhood in communist Romania where rules were often there (obviously) to control and oppress and not to support, and where common sense and humanity were seen as bugs in a system designed to dehumanize.

I became deeply suspicious of any organization where employees have no voice or where change from the inside is not possible.

And yet, I am also a big believer in organizations as places of collaboration. We can do so many things together that we cannot do on our own. So this is why I embarked on this professional journey, to help people in organizations liberate their spirit and power at work, for all our benefit.

I recognize my own struggle in many of my clients.

They try; they fail. Then they try harder and keep at it. If too much is not working, they start to look for a new job. If that happens repeatedly, I notice in them a sense of resignation, exhaustion, sometimes even burnout. Some of them will go on an internal exile and put their energy in projects outside of work, to make up for their sense of waste and insignificance. If they have any energy and time left because they are busy, very busy, only not with the kind of work that makes their heart sing.

Some of them are on the verge of giving up. They have given up hope that it can be any different in an organizational setting. They toy with the idea of leaving and creating their own business. That is sometimes a good idea, but often, not an option (or not a viable one). This waste of energy and potential makes me sad. It doesn't have to be this way.

To find out what works, I have studied many success stories (mine and the ones of my clients), so I know that they exist!

Of course, succeeding means different things for different people. For those who look for more traditional career advancement, this book might not be the right one. The advice that you receive here can surely help get you to your next job with more power and clout, but this is not the main goal. Most of the people I coach are looking to transform their environment into one that is more open, receptive, and supportive to new ideas. A more flexible, human environment where ideas and new initiative have a better life expectancy and the chance to flourish.

Some of my clients have a very specific purpose; they seek to realize a specific dream, a specific project, an innovation maybe, a better way of doing things. They are ambitious, but not for titles or climbing the corporate ladder. Nor they are averse to it—it's just not their main driver. They are ambitious to contribute, to realize meaningful work and make the vision of their company a reality. They are creative and resourceful, and when they succeed, it is a sight to behold. Some of the most transformative initiatives for companies came about this way; and on their way, they gained supporters. Their initial ideas improve further, as do their skills of bringing them into the world. I have seen people and organizations uplifted and transformed by such successful initiatives.

One common thing about these success stories is that they are not obvious. They are beyond just somebody performing their tasks well. These examples are people who had an idea that went beyond their job description and their formal power in the company: their idea presented challenges, sometimes to the narrow way of doing things in one particular project, and sometimes to the fundamental way the company was seeking to achieve its goals.

I conclude that the people who succeed need special equipment. They need some protective gear, they need special high-energy astronaut food to keep them going, they need good tools to cut through the weeds, a compass, and good communication tools. These are all metaphors, of course, for the concrete (but flexible) roadmap, ideas, tools, tips, and guidance that you can get in the pages of this book.

I am writing it for my people, the ones that will show up every day with hope and courage and determination. If you are one of them, welcome, and keep reading. I seek to make you more effective and successful because your spirit is a treasure to cherish and uplift, and by being successful and ultimately visible you will empower other people to do the same. We are living in times when we can't afford to silence our collective problem-solving skills, constructive ideas, and any type of contributions that bring more life and joy. So, let's not.

Chapter 3

Roadmap

I have studied, observed, and advised change agents, intrapreneurs, and all kinds of corporate rebels for years by now.
My research questions were: What makes them successful?
What differentiates them from know-betters and change
theorists that all companies have plenty of? What do they have
in common?

These are important questions for me, too, because they tell
me what the success factors are and how can I help them to do
more of what matters to their success.

Of course, they are as diverse as they can be. Their ideas
for change are different, their level in the hierarchy of their

organization is different, they are men and women, and they come from different countries. Also, they operate in vastly different organizations, some of them in huge supranational institutions, others in smaller governmental agencies. Some of them work in international or local N.G.O.s, middle size companies, branches of multinationals or huge company headquarters.

Many people that approach me feel that they are operating in uncharted territory without a compass, exposed to the total randomness of the elements and (almost) without any power to guide themselves toward their goal. It is a question of luck, of hit and miss. They feel that they don't have much control over whether their ideas and their contribution will travel anywhere, whether they will be heard, or whether they can have any impact. So, they consider moving to another job, another unit. Essentially consider finding another boss that is more open, curious and welcoming of innovation.

In the pages of this book, I bring together for you what works. I have learned that a systematic approach is possible. There are steps anybody can take. Sometimes this approach will yield the desired impact very fast, sometimes it will take time, and it will take perseverance. Sometimes you will need to pursue all the steps intently, like a project manager, some other times it will suffice to invite gently, hold, and let unfold, more like a midwife helping along a natural process of birth.

All the parts of this process can be pursued in many different ways. I provided you methodologies that I know to work very well, but they are not the only ones possible. Whenever you have good and proven resources, proven ways of achieving the same, use them.

So, without further ado, here is an overview of what it takes to bring your innovation and ideas to your company, and make your organization listen and change.

1. From rebel to intrapreneur

"Intrapreneurship" is the act of behaving like an entrepreneur while working within a large organization.

I found that the effective change agents in the organizations that I know have an amazing entrepreneurial spirit... and instead of opposing and resisting, they learn to engage, to play with the actors in the system.

The first and most important step is to become the person who can actually lead this process of transformation. It is easy to have an opinion and to stand in opposition but to take the lead, recognize the power that you already have right now, and use it, that is hard. Nobody can stop you at this stage but yourself. This is all about personal development and it is the most important, and arguably more difficult part of the process. Head to Chapter 4 for ways to get yourself started and plenty of tools that you can use to develop your personal leadership skills.

2. Better together

Organizational transformation and significant impact is not something you are likely to achieve on your own, not even if you are the C.E.O., and even much less if you don't have a formal mandate and lots of formal power. Find and build your team that will amplify your effort, your impact, and multiply your reach and your intelligence. This team will be the cradle of the lasting change that you are envisioning. Chapter 5 is all about how to find your team members and how to turn yourselves into a team.

3. Build your movement

Whatever it is that you are pioneering, you want to be in conversation with those around you who have a stake in what you also care about. Some of them will recognize what you are offering, and they will be your early clients, users, champions, and supporters. They are your movement, a movement that advances your collective purpose. You will learn about how to invite, incubate, and nurture your movement in Chapter 6.

4. Sponsorship

In a traditionally structured organization, you cannot achieve a significant impact and lasting change without support from the hierarchy. Not everybody has to support your ideas, but you need help, and to let your team see beyond what you get from spearheading your movement. Who are the right people? And how will they come on board? Once they have offered their support how do you keep them on board? And how exactly can they support your cause? Finding sponsors in a hierarchical organization is key to success, and I devote Chapter 7 to telling you exactly how to do it.

5. **Prototyping**

Whether you want to champion a new approach, a process, a concrete project or a product, you cannot assume and expect to have it perfect right from the beginning.

You will be better, smarter, and better adapted if you test your ideas in action. You will reduce the risks and increase the chances of success by creating experiments, testing your assumptions, and continuously learning.

Nothing brings more energy and satisfaction than action, and prototyping will get you in action fast. It will deliver new experiences, fast learning, and new perspectives.

6. **Changing the organizational story**

Last but not least, if you want your proposals to stick you will need to anchor it into the organizational narrative and have a supportive organizational culture. Changing organizational culture is difficult, but you and your movement can (and better do) play a role in shaping it. In Chapter 9 I will suggest several methodologies that you can use to do just that.

I will talk about each of those steps with details on approach and methodology. If you have already started, and already accomplished some steps, I still recommend that you read those chapters. You might get useful ideas and perspectives regardless. You don't need to read the following chapters necessarily in any order. While they have a logic to them these steps can also work independently.

The only one you cannot at all disregard is the first step, Chapter 4.

At the end of the day, you yourself are the biggest asset and could be the biggest roadblock for pursuing your vision and achieving your goals.

The Jedi Art of Summoning the Force

"We must become the change we want to see in the world."
– Mahatma Gandhi

I f you are staring incredulously at the title of this chapter, let me explain: beyond luck and circumstance (and without diminishing the role they play) I have seen quiet, unassuming people pull off amazing, transformational successes in small and big organizations, sometimes even transforming oppressive political systems.

The ones in the public sphere are known (think of Malalas, Harvey Milks, Gandhis, and Nelson Mandelas of this world—and we have them in all countries). The ones operating in the corporate environment are less well-known, but they exist and they do amazing things.

What distinguishes them is indeed a level of personal development: they have mastered the art of knowing themselves and have arrived at a place of inner confidence and quiet courage of their convictions that is the source of their power and their strength.

They know how to summon "the Force" (or in more down-to-earth terms, they know how to get things done) that will change the world around them.

Doing this is not some elite talent, granted as a birth-right to selected few. This is a set of practices that we can all also do: we can all be Jedi in practice. In the words of American writer Will Durant, "We are what we repeatedly do. Excellence, then, is not an act but a habit."

The Importance of Inner Space

In a recent interview, Sara Blakey the C.E.O. of Spanx said, "Your negative self-talk is the No. 1 barrier to success." Now you might think that this is a phrase from somebody who is so successful that surely she has amazing possibilities from where she sits. She can "afford" to be positive. But she is definitely onto something. Some of my clients, talented and brilliant people, hit a wall when I talk to them about the importance of their thoughts and feelings, what I call the inner space. They label it as New Age and think it is a waste of time and resources to explore and overcome their inner stumbling blocks and sabotage patterns.

They want tips and tricks, but I am here to tell you that all the tips and tricks in the world are worth nothing if you keep yourself from actually implementing any of it, or when you sabotage yourself. You must align yourself; getting your inner self ready for the success that you want to create is the number one predictor of this success, regardless of the environment in which you operate.

How do you do that? By becoming conscious of your own thought patterns and triggers, understanding them and changing them if they are not serving you anymore. This is, of course, easier said than done. Changing ingrained thought patterns is the most challenging work there is. It is also the most important and the ultimate success factor in projects large and small, professional and personal. If you are creating something that is in its first manifestation an expression of yourself, then it will carry some of your mental patterns into the world, just as a child of yours would carry your genes.

The good news is you have more control over your thoughts than over your genes, and you can set yourself and your project up for success. This chapter is about that. Working on your own internal space is not preparation for the work; it is the work. It is arguably the most important part of the work because it is through this that you will become the intrapreneur, the person who has what it takes in resourcefulness, resilience, courage, and risk-taking to create beyond what is expected of you.

This is leadership work and it has nothing to do with a formal title in your organization. It is a leadership work that you will need to work into. As Warren G. Bennis says, "The most dangerous leadership myth is that leaders are born—that there is a genetic factor to leadership. This myth asserts that people simply either have certain charismatic qualities or not. That's nonsense; in fact, the opposite is true. Leaders are made rather than born."

Making it Your Job

The successful intrapreneurs that I met are a very diverse group. Some of them are extroverts that can fill a room with their presence, but many are not. Many of my clients with the most impressive records are quiet and even introverted people. They are women and men, their careers are diverse and not linear, and they have overcome difficulties and setbacks. They still do every day. Just because they now know how to create and deliver really impactful change does not mean there is no resistance left or that nothing will fail them anymore. They still have doubts and questions and dilemmas. All of it. But they have one thing in common. All of them. They are thoroughly committed to their vision and have taken upon themselves the responsibility to make it happen. They have made it their jobs, even if according to their job description it might not be (indeed in many cases it goes well beyond what they are required and expected to do). In some cases, it is actually their job, but the creative approach that they are proposing raises brows and resistance with their management. This decisiveness and commitment set them apart from the legions of people who complain about all kinds of stuff. At any moment in the cafeteria, by the water cooler, or in meetings you'll easily find people who are dissatisfied. Some things (or many things) don't work the way they expect, or desire: work processes are not efficient, resources are wasted, management is bad, priorities are not clear. Scores of well-meaning people in the company have "ideas" about how to make improvements but have abdicated any responsibility (beyond their normal task) to actually improve things. Somebody else should do that, the leadership, the managers, the people who are actually paid (handsomely) to do this.

I have sympathy for these arguments; so many people have bought into the story of their powerlessness and insignificance that they have given up any attempts to change things. Many others just don't really care so much, really not. Their attention and commitment are somewhere else. But every once in a while, someone will just take up a challenge and make it their job to improve something, or change, or accomplish something new. They have a vision, they are inspired. They take upon themselves something that is (safe to say) not the path of least resistance. I found that this is the most important prerequisite to success. Yes, there are means and tools to be effective, but unless you are fully committed to your goal, your project, it will not work.

If you are the one holding this vision before anybody else (or anybody else in your organization), if you are not fully committed, that will show up in the DNA of the project... and other people will not commit either. And if nobody cares, nothing happens.

Your own commitment comes before anything else.

Your Why

Clarifying why you care about it enough to drive a change or innovation is very important and comes hand in hand with your commitment. What is behind your choice to put your energy precisely here? I found that people are driven by a mix of excitement, inspiration, and the sense of dissatisfaction with the status quo. Not only a general dissatisfaction but a personal one. They feel they are personally stuck, they are not using their potential, they are wasting their lives and resources. They feel they are not living up to their values. When they connect to an idea that inspires them, it is more than just a good idea, more than just random innovation. It is an opportunity to leave a mark, to bring more of their resources to work. An opportunity to be more true to themselves, and impact their environment.

What is your motivation? Why do you choose this particular battle to fight? Clarity about what is behind it will give you the necessary energy to go on when it is not easy, and also the necessary information to know when to quit. Even if a project is ultimately doable, even if a battle is ultimately winnable, it might not be worth the cost. Like entrepreneurs working in their own business, sometimes you lose, sometimes it is wiser to give up. But if you are to stand any chance for success, at any moment you have to take responsibility for it and to know why you are doing it.

There are many negative motivators in the organization. The positive ones can be extrinsic, such as the hope for career advancement, better exposure, and more money. There can also be an intrinsic inspiration, which is the internal need to make a difference. This inspiration can come from a particular product or idea, commitment to a vision of the world, your values. My experience is that you cannot run on extrinsic motivators alone. If you do, your intrapreneurial project is at risk of you dropping it as soon as you don't need it anymore for your promotion, or as soon as it gets some blowback or displeases higher-ups. Which it will. An organization is a complex organism, and you ought to bump into resistance and ruffled egos. Conviction and commitment to what is right and important to you can pull you through, and more importantly, can support the people that you will attract around your project.

So ask yourself the following questions: Why do I want to do this? What part of me will be expressed through this? What of my dearly held values will I express?

And also contemplate the alternative of not doing it, after all, starting but not completing may leave you even more depressed and frustrated. How would you feel about yourself if you are not pursuing this? How would you feel about your job? Can you not do it? This last question might feel superfluous because of course, we can always not do something, we always have a choice. But I found that many of my clients, just like many entrepreneurs feel that deep down they have to go for it if they are to live up to the image they have of themselves.

Once you have clarified your personal stake, it is time to reflect on the organizational "why". Why is it important and urgent to make that change or implement that initiative that you are proposing? This is the first time of many when you get to reflect about this, but you'll create a more secure footing for yourself if you clarify the "why" of your organization right from the start.

How does your proposal fit with the work of your organization in the world?

How does it fit with its values and its mission? Sometimes, or pretty often, there is a great difference the stated values of an organization and what you experience. This is a source of tension and maybe you can contribute to clarifying the gap with your work.

Keep in mind that even if you have a clear idea about those benefits, this questioning is something that you will need to repeat with every new person that will join your quest. Their perspective is just as important and needs to be included. It will not be your vision alone.

Fear

Creating something new, stepping up in a different way, involves certain risks (above all the risk of being seen as out of your line, above your pay grade, or critical of the status quo). These risks will alarm all of your defense mechanisms designed to keep you safe. Your internal worrier will stand right up in its chair and wrestle for the controls of your mind. If you have seen the Pixar movie *Inside Out*, then you have a good picture for that.

The emotion Fear will do with everything in its power to stop you from doing what it perceives to be a dangerous act. Indeed it tries to protect you. For most of human history, people were not able to choose their communities. They were born or socialized within one, and their survival depended on being accepted as part of this community. So this fear of being judged and rejected by your peers has a very clear developmental, protective purpose.

Yet in this situation, it may be overreacting. Your thoughts might tell you that your livelihood is under threat. They might tell you that you will be ridiculed and derided by your peers and people above you in the pecking order. You might fear that standing up and out for something will take so much effort and time from you that you will ruin your private life. You might worry that your initiative or ideas will ultimately fail and that it's going to impact your career chances.

You might suffer, like all high achievers, from imposter syndrome. Fearing that you will be exposed as a fraud, that people will ultimately see that you are not perfect and you don't have the answer to all the questions at your fingertips.

I want you to know that your fears are trying to protect you. Most of them are exaggerated and even as you learn good strategies to prepare for success, more importantly, you have to learn to manage the fear. There's always going to be a certain amount of risk, and this is a central part of intrapreneurship and innovation. You can risk mitigate and risk manage many things, but there will always be things that your mind will blow out of proportion to keep you from doing what it perceives to be threatening. You simply cannot innovate, create, step up and feel no fear at all.

Courage is not the absence of fear, but rather feeling the fear and going ahead anyway. One step at a time, gathering enough strength to move in the direction that you desire. If you do you will build up your confidence and you will feel more powerful with time. Some of the things that terrify you now will not be scary at all, but just normal. Yet there will always be new things that stretch your resolve and trigger your fear and you will have to step through them. The only way to go forward is… to go forward. If you wait for the fear to pass or to become confident before you act, then it will not happen. Confidence and the sense of your own power will come from your experience of having mastered some tasks that are scary or difficult for you, not by thinking about them. No amount of waiting or thinking about it can replace the action.

I remember when I started to work with groups some twenty-five years ago, I was terrified of speaking in front of them. I was worried that I would not sound smart enough, that my peers would laugh, that my participants would not take me seriously. I was worried that I would be exposed for not actually knowing well enough what I'm doing. I was working at the Council of Europe with simultaneous translation, and I was so stressed that I kept scratching the microphone, much to the stress of the interpreteurs in the booths, tasked with translating what I was saying. To this day I feel for the interpreters who had to put up with that. My colleagues brought me a stress ball to calm down. The only way of conquering this fear was to keep doing it. To do it often, to get used to it, and to get comfortable with it.

It also wasn't great right from the beginning. I got feedback on how to improve on everything. My voice, my posture. There was no way I could prepare for everything I would ever have to say. Not even everything I had to say in one single training session. So I prepared the best I could and then went for it. This is how I conquered my fear. Of course, public speaking is a skill anyone can master, but the same is true for any idea that exposes you as different and maybe a little (or very) unorthodox.

Any new idea can be seen as a challenge to the status quo and we can rightly expect that not everybody will embrace it. So while many of your fears are most probably overblown I don't want to say they are completely wrong either. But I want to call on your courage and bravery. There will always be some degree of worry and fear (otherwise you'd be a psychopath) and you can do great things nevertheless. The great majority of work-related things that scare you today will lose their grip on you and you will be free to walk on and do the things you most desire.

We'll go right on to talk about ways to get on the top of all the angst and drama, but at least some degree of discomfort is not avoidable. Look at it as a sign of growth. Embrace it and move forward. Your path to success leads right through it.

Limiting Beliefs

Einstein once said, "The mind is a wonderful servant but a very poor master." He had great intelligence, so he obviously wasn't complaining about that. Rather, he was referring to every brain's tendency to go into energy-saving mode, work out patterns, and deploy them at certain signals, circumventing energy consuming decision making mechanisms. This is, of course, also survival mechanism, and an important function of the brain: learning from our experiences and experiences of others to avoid danger.

When we are in a survival situation, natural or social, it serves us well to identify the smallest signs of danger unconsciously and avoid them. But not all that triggers the danger signals represents a real danger. We feel some fear of the unknown of being exposed and excluded, and we tell ourselves a story about why this all makes sense. We rationalize the fear with a story about great danger and thus we intensify the fear even further until it becomes so gripping that we cannot move anymore. Our mind has taken control of the situation and successfully avoided the perceived danger.

Yet a lot of the stories that we tell ourselves will not stand in close-up scrutiny. If we approach them consciously and shine a light on them, we can stop the thought train that scares us and holds us back from something that we really want.

How to do that? The first step is to observe. Our thoughts are triggered automatically and it all goes so fast we might not be at all conscious of them. So, when you notice that you are acting against what you actually want to achieve it is time to slow down and analyze what is actually happening.

Our mind has a great skill to cover its tracks. So, often you will find one story buried in another story. For example, you know that you should create a presentation, a proposal for an idea. Or maybe you need to talk to some new people about it and you are worried about their reactions. You are telling yourself that speaking about is risky and they won't like it anyway.

This is a limiting belief because you don't know how the people will actually react to your proposal before you ask and there are good chances that if you would be willing and open to accept some rejection, you would get also significant support. To help you deal with this discomfort, you might have devised a secondary story that could sound like this: *I can't do this because it is June and everybody is very busy at the closing of the financial year. It is not a good time. I will wait until the end of September.* Or, *I heard that the leadership might be changing soon, so I will wait and see what happens there and when this is clear then I'll start talking to people.* Or, *I need a new degree first, otherwise, I am not qualified to talk about this problem. Unfortunately, now is not the right time for studies either.*

These are thoughts that are meant to deflect and protect you from the discomfort of having to deal with your primary issue. It gives you something else to work on to keep you busy. It gives you something else you can fail at that you can blame on circumstances or other people.

The good news is, you can get on top of your limiting beliefs and you can master dealing with them. This is a skill like any other and you can learn it. When you get good at it you become a Jedi, because your many superpowers will be set free. This, of course, sounds like hyperbole but truly being able to become the master of your thoughts, not their slave, is likely the most significant thing you can do for your success.

These are several very good self-inquiry tools that can help you identify a thought that is limiting and replace it with another one that is more helpful and just as true. The most well-known is from the "Work of Byron Katie," a beautiful and elegant inquiry system that allows us to loosen the grip of some thoughts that feel true, but only until we really look at them. I whole-heartedly recommend you explore her work, as it is the most powerful tool to create consciousness and space between you and your thoughts, so that you can decide what is true and what is helpful and not be triggered into an automatic reaction that takes your agency away.

I will talk about another method that I found to be a little more accessible. It is called "The Self-Coaching Model" and it comes from the work of Brooke Castillo. It asks you for some mental gymnastics to separate the thought you have from the actual circumstance behind it.

The circumstances are the facts, the simple facts with no judgment or qualifier attached to them. So a fact would be "my proposal was rejected".

But this circumstance triggers, in a split second, an entire train of thoughts and consequences. For example, my thought will be: "I have failed" or "I cannot innovate here." This thought makes me feel the emotions sad, worried, unconfident in my ability to succeed. The emotion in its turn will lead to action: minimize risks and exposure, keep my head down, do things that I know for sure that will succeed (aka no new things). This action will create the result that "proves" my thoughts right. I have failed, I cannot innovate here.

Brooke Castillo describes a very clear chain of events:

- Circumstances trigger thoughts
- Thoughts create emotions
- Emotions will determine actions
- Actions will create results
- The results will *always* confirm the thought

According to Brooke Castillo's Self-Coaching Model the action that we take will always prove the thought that was at its source. But here is also where our greatest power lies. If we manage to consciously choose our thoughts we will have created different emotions, actions, and different results that will prove the (more helpful) thought that we chose.

So if instead of thinking "I have failed; I cannot innovate here," I choose the thought "I tried," or "I demonstrated that I care and have new ideas," or "I proved that I am not afraid to take risks." My emotion for this will be pride and confidence. I will

feel more motivated to rework my proposal or improve it, and to look for support so that it gets approved. The result might very well be that it does get approved. But whatever happens, my thought that "I am a risk taker and an innovator" will be proven right. I might not be able to change a particular instance but I can change and choose my thoughts.

Let's look at my client Steven as an example. He wasn't happy with some consultative meetings organized by his department because of the way they were run. He found them boring, pointless, and badly organized. They weren't conducive to an ideal collaboration and were a waste of everybody's time. The problem was that beyond being boring, the lack of actual good collaboration was directly impacting his ability to do his work. Steven was also quite excited to try some new things, to shake up and change the format of the meetings, to invite some new stakeholders into the room, and to use the time to much better effect. He knew that many of his colleagues were also dissatisfied with meetings but many of them could not envision anything better.

In a big governmental body people almost expected meetings to be boring, but Steven had this vision of having all the people in the room bringing in their experiences and perspectives and talking openly and freely about how to solve some of the common challenges. He had the vision of people leaving energized and excited, of friendships being started, of great ideas and projects emerging, and of a resulting commitment to achieving action. He had the vision of what would be possible if they changed how the meetings were set up and run.

Yet, when I met Steven he wasn't really doing anything about it. He told me that his boss would never approve of those changes because they were a little unorthodox and "New Age-y."

To achieve the excitement and collaboration he wanted, Steven knew he needed to propose some big changes to the format of the meeting. They needed to let go of the predefined results, the choreographed to the last detail program. They had to change the setting of the room. They needed some additional resources for the meetings to have some external support. That felt like a very big risk. Steven told himself that his ideas would never fly and that the people in his meetings, an international group of financial controllers, were not used to open exchanges. They might react badly, he feared. At least some of them would.

In conversations, it emerged that behind all of those fears there was also something else. While he wanted to innovate, he was also worried about raising expectations and then failing. Not being able to deliver on his vision might damage his reputation for years to come. That fear was preventing him from any move and he had to tackle it before he could move on to anything else.

His thoughts were obvious:

- It is too risky to try a new thing
- There will be a backlash
- People will hate it
- He will lose everything

But what were the actual facts, the circumstances behind it? The facts were people complain about the meeting, and in the past, some of the new initiatives had failed but also some had succeeded. When he thought those things about the given circumstances Steven felt fear and lack of confidence, which is not surprising given the scary picture he painted. From this emotion, he chose not to go ahead with his proposal in order to keep himself safe. It makes sense, it is a survival strategy.

This action, or in this case inaction, led to the situation continuing on as it was, a result that very well confirmed the thought that Steven had. Such a change will never work, people are not used to this kind of change. The final result of having this thought will always confirm the thought because we will work unconsciously to prove ourselves right much harder than we will work to achieve the result we ultimately desire. We will invest a lot of energy in proving our limiting beliefs right.

But here is the good news. While we might not be able to choose a different set of circumstances, we can choose a thought that will be as true for us as the limiting beliefs, but it is better because it creates a better result.

Our Steven can choose to think that people appreciate quality and great meetings. That would be just as true. His people like when meetings are well prepared and well organized. When he thinks these thoughts, Steven feels excited because he knows that he can actually deliver a much better-organized meeting with many collaborative elements and much better results. The action that he will take is to initiate such a pilot meeting, make a good case for it, and then prepare it very well. He will still feel jitters, be a little nervous, but the meeting will be a success because it is well prepared. This is his result. People will appreciate the well-prepared meeting, the result that proves his thought.

Steven has learned a lot in the process. He learned from the preparation, he learned how to better and more efficiently prepare next time. He has more actual data about how his group reacts to this kind of innovation. He sounds more capable and confident. The results of this meeting were better and its results made his next report. A much more meaningful and pointed report than what he could produce before. His direct boss who was skeptical at the beginning was finally convinced by the great feedback of the participants. Now he's cautiously supporting Steven to repeat this experience and better understands the need for preparation and more resources such as a bigger room. Some of the participants approach Steven and ask his support and advice for approving their own meetings. Now Steven sits at the center of what could be a movement for a better meeting with far-reaching impact on how people feel at work and on the results of their work.

All it took was to pick a different thought. In Henry Ford's famous words, "Whether you think you can or you think you can't, you're right." The thought will create the results that confirm it. Yet I know this does not come easily to many of us. If we are not used to consciously following our train of thought then we lose the chance to actually decide what to think. The situation, the circumstance will trigger a thought within a split second and then we will be on our way to working diligently to confirm it. Victor Frankl, the famous psychologist and Holocaust survivor, said about our power to choose, "Between stimulus there is a space. In this space lie our power and our freedom." This is exactly what he meant. We have the freedom to pick our response, our own reaction, but only if we are aware of what we are doing because it happens so fast.

I recommend that you make a daily practice of it. Every time that you observe yourself thinking thoughts that keep you back from doing what you want have a little moment of reckoning.

What is the circumstance? What is my thought? Can I pick a thought that is more helpful, that does not rob me of my power, my agency *and* that is also true?

You get better at this and it is a lifelong practice. You will be able to free yourself from many self-imposed limitations you may not be even aware of. You will be free to create much more of what you desire.

Negative Self-Talk

What we think about a circumstance defines our actions and our results. The thoughts we have about ourselves are probably the most important part of these limiting beliefs. For one, they're pervasive. We evaluate our own performance, look, and circumstances all the time. We more often than not tend to be our harshest judges. Nobody, certainly none of my clients, wants to be a narcissist devoid of any critical self-awareness, but the relentless internal criticism and skepticism that we deliver unto ourselves diminish and demoralize us. We are always listening to this critical voice, much more accustomed to judgment than to praise and validation.

This is not objective feedback. It is a put down that lacks love and compassion. We would never talk to other people like that and in most places that would be not acceptable and deemed highly offensive.

Picking more useful thoughts about ourselves to replace the barrage of internal criticism is probably one of the most important practices of all. Learn to think "I can figure this out" instead of "I have no idea how to do this;" "I am resourceful" instead of "I am a fraud;" "I am a human in all its glory" instead of "I am never enough because I am not perfect;" "I have tried and learned" instead of "I have failed miserably." This can make all the difference to who we become and what can we achieve in the world.

The key to this is consciousness, eavesdropping on our own thoughts, knowing that they are not the truth, they contain judgments and evaluations that are often not accurate. Giving ourselves the chance to pick new thoughts about ourselves and others can help yield better results. When we are kinder to ourselves, we can relax and exit the constant fight-or-flight emergency mode, and we can be more creative. If we are more loving toward ourselves we will take better care of ourselves, grant ourselves more resources and support. The results will be much better, and we will be happier.

Linking it back to being a successful intrapreneur, confidence and resilience are key attributes to any entrepreneurial journey. We cannot rely on luck alone to create good conditions for us. That would mean waiting and wasting our resources. Putting ourselves down prevents us also from learning and doing better next time. If we see ourselves as a failure, not able to take distance from a situation and better evaluate the dynamics of it, we will only confirm the bias that we have, and not learn anything new.

I recommend that you observe yourself for one day and make note of all the things you tell yourself about yourself, good or bad. There are so many thoughts, you won't be able to capture all of them, but try to catch a sample. Are you happy with what you see? How would you like anybody to talk that way to your child, spouse, or any other beloved person? This is your test. If you would not allow anybody to talk in this tone of voice to your significant others, then you should definitely not be talking like that to yourself.

Listen intently, and when you hear the self-bashing, stop, let it go, don't blame and criticize yourself for doing it, just let it go. Pick another thought instead. Think of all the obstacles you've overcome and the things that you are amazing at and refer to them. "I am resourceful," "I can do hard things," "I can bring joy to this task."

Try it for one day, just one day, see how you feel.

I warn you that even trying it for a day is not easy, especially if you are used to talking down to yourself. Unless it is a perfect day surrounded only by lovely people at their very best, things will happen that will trigger your usual thinking. So do take extra attention and effort and when you catch yourself, stop. Start again.

I also recommend that you look into support, like coaching. You can plow through it alone, or you can work with somebody who knows how to support you, to get through your blockades, and help you progress much faster. Investing in yourself is important, and one of my top recommendations for intrapreneurs, if you are working to create a movement of change and support, you need somebody at your back. I find in my work that a lot of senior managers and CEOs find it easier to welcome this notion. Maybe because they have budgets allocated to such purposes.

Even if you are not in the top leadership, organizing your support is among the most important strategies you can learn from them. Check your limiting thoughts on the topic of access to support or time. Once you get past them, you will see that there are possibilities, some of them within your organization, some of them outside.

Your limiting beliefs, your personal drama, fear, and worry will never be completely out of the picture, even when you have become much better about uplifting yourself instead of putting yourself down. They are part of our human experience, and among the most resilient ones for that, so you will have to learn to act with them by your side.

Find Your Power

To act despite fear, you will have to build up your power and sense of confidence. Nothing gives you more of a boost than to actually succeed at doing things that you found challenging and being recognized for them.

In my work with organizations, I often notice a sense of lack of agency. We expect others, the system, the leadership, the management, the members to change while giving up our own agency to create any change. This surrendering of responsibility and the sense of powerlessness that comes with it is very human. But remember, you made this transformation your job. You took it, now you will want to do it, and you will have to build up your sense of power and agency so that you can actually move and create change.

Power is often derided (by the ones who are oppressed) like a destructive force, and not completely without reason. Being in a position and a situation of power for a long time skews perception, and change is a way people think. It makes them more confident, obviously, more likely to take risks, but less empathic and less able to relate to others. It can create some kind of tunnel vision, a focus on the goal without consideration of the consequences or casualties.

The opposite of this feeling, powerlessness, is just as damaging. It will lead to apathy, lack of engagement or anger. People who don't feel powerful will be more empathic towards the perspective and the suffering of others, but without a sense of power and agency we will not trust ourselves to direct projects to success, and we will be scared to take any risks. I see this in organizations all the time. Employees feeling powerless to change anything will complain and blame, but not take any responsibility. They will expect all the initiative to come from their hierarchy.

The two perspectives feed each other. The higher management will be confirmed in its belief that they are deservedly special and in a position of power because they are the only ones who can drive initiatives to success. The employees will be confirmed in their beliefs that they have no power to change anything, and nobody wants to listen to them. They will not even try. If you recognize any of that in your workplace, know that you are not confined to one single perspective. You can actually increase your power and agency. If you are in a position of power, you can certainly become more informed, connected, and all-around better leader if you allow yourself to experience other perspectives, too.

But how do you increase your power? I am not talking about the formal power in organizations. That may follow, but this is not what I am talking about here. You can change how you feel, your sense of power and sense of confidence, and that will impact your ability to initiate and drive your ideas ahead. You can do that consciously, going out of your comfort zone and mastering challenges. Some of them will be squarely in your professional realm, so you don't need anybody's approval to become even better at what you do. Some of the challenges have to do with how you show up in meetings, in front of your peers and management. You will have to get into the habit of speaking up and sharing your contribution, which may be a challenge at first, but the only way to build up confidence and a sense of power is to go out of your comfort zone and build up a string of successes. Success and recognition will give you a sense of power and ability.

What are the areas where you feel right now most at ease and in your element, where you feel happy and confident in your work? Give yourself a set of challenges to build on that, to increase it. Also, share your ideas with people who are generally sympathetic to these ideas, and you know that they would listen and could support them. People who support your ideas and understand them are better suited for this purpose than people who are generally your friends and family. The latter may feel very protective of you and can stop you in your tracks if, out of love, they will talk you out of any risk-taking.

Present your ideas several times and ask for feedback. Through feedback, you will receive valuable information. Not necessarily about the content of your ideas. That is, of course, possible, too, but certainly about how other people will think.

When hearing your ideas, especially when they are unusual or innovative, many people will be triggered and they will unload on you their limiting beliefs. This will help build up your case and give you information about how to socialize your ideas and initiatives to assorted audiences. After you have talked more about your idea, you will feel more and more confident to do so again. Stepping up this work more and more visibly, you will be triggered again and again. Your limited beliefs will come to you in full swing. If you want to succeed, you will have to be able to deal with your internal drama. Otherwise, you will sabotage yourself and stop before you achieve your goal.

Taking responsibility, tackling your limiting beliefs, and building up your sense of confidence and power is an ongoing practice. As I said at the beginning of this chapter, this is not preparatory work. This is already the work of the intrapreneur before you can create the externally visible results. We often make the mistake of going straight out into the world, but we not ready to drive our ideas to success. If you are making the internal work an integral part of the work you have to do, you will have the energy and the resilience to make a success of it.

Chapter 5

Your Start-Up Team

"People are the most important thing. Business model and product will follow if you have the right people."
— **Adam Newmann**, co-founder of We Work

We are familiar from the popular culture with the image of the hero, the savior who will single-handedly solve problems, win battles, lead companies and nations to succeed. In business, the image of the rock star entrepreneur who will bootstrap their idea and then take it to dazzling success underscores the myth of the one lonely and brilliant leader.

This myth is outdated in most circumstances but especially so when you are trying to achieve success in the complex and fraught environment of a company. It is misleading and disempowering… let go of it!

Your chances of success are significantly higher if you don't go it alone. To build support for your vision you have to have colleagues.

A transformational, innovative project like yours requires collective leadership, not an individual. That does not diminish your leadership one bit but adds strength, vitality, and traction to your work.

Who Are My People? Where Is My Team?

Look for them among the people who are excited by your ideas already. I can almost guarantee that unless you are advocating from some truly outlandish proposal there are already people in your company who resonate with it. They will be your colleagues, your tribe. I use the term start-up team to underline the entrepreneurial aspect of your initiative. You act as an entrepreneur (intrapreneur!) and you champion and "bring to market" a new idea.

The start-up team is your initial team of people who will co-create this endeavor with you.

Find them and invite them into open conversations about this vision and your idea.

This is the first step.

You will do the same as what you would do if you would seek to build a team for your business idea. You are in the "garage" phase here, you need people who are excited and hungry for the change that you are championing. Find them.

The start-up team, the first group of people who are joining with you in the endeavor are essential. They will collaborate with you on improving the original initiative, prototyping it and sharing it with their colleagues.

What kind of people should you invite? People you can trust but are not necessarily your best friends. Certainly not (only) your direct reports. You want to have people from a variety of perspectives with a variety of skills who can bring many different skills and gifts to improve your proposal.

First, you invite them to an exploratory conversation with you, to see if your ideas truly resonate and if you have a shared vision about what is possible.

Only if they feel like "Oh, *YES!*" and if they are excited and enthusiastic, will you want them on your team.

As you will see in this book, there is a lot to do to champion an idea in an organization. It is not a passive "wait to be discovered" type of approach. The start-up team is at the center of it all. These are the people who need to share a commitment and they will have to be motivated just as you are, by their deep belief that what you seek to do is right and valuable.

Unlike in start-ups that are not embedded in an organization, the people that you invite will likely not be motivated by the promise of fast financial success. They might even perceive joining your team as a distraction from their career. Strong, intrinsic motivation is essential. You can use the steps in this book as a blueprint for the kind of work that they would be engaging in. The details, of course, would be co-created step-by-step, but it should be clear that you've invited them to a long-standing commitment, not a one-off.

Not everybody will say yes.

People will react to such an invitation in different ways. Some will be happy to join into your venture while some will be hesitant. They all bring to the table their own egos and questions and limiting beliefs. So the reasons for refusing to join you may reflect many things that are not necessarily their opinion about your proposal. However, it is your work to create the kind of good invitation from your heart that will give the people inspiration but also an opportunity to identify themselves with it and contribute to it.

No matter how great your proposal is if you can't share the ownership of it with others who can fully participate to develop it with you, chances are that people will not be excited to join. After all, if it is your work alone and an expression of yourself alone, why would they invest time and energy to bring it forward? If, however, they can shape the ideas and proposals according to their own angles and perspectives, their stake in it will be real.

The two essentials that I mention here are inviting and hosting the co-creative conversations. Let's take them one by one.

The Invitation

The way you invite these people to join you at this early stage of creating your team sets the tone and the energy of the entire initiative. Long before people actually join you in conversation you have already thought about and appreciated their work and contribution and their potential support. You had a dream about what it could mean for you, for them, the entire company and ultimately your clients if they would join your quest and share your vision. The invitation needs to honor that. The spirit of cooperation and co-creation starts with the invitation.

In the organizational practice inviting people to meetings and conversations has been degraded to the calendar invites and Outlook invites. You need to go beyond that. In this stage, meet the first people of your start-up team personally and initiate deeper meaningful conversations with them. Share your heart, your story, your vision. Inquire and deeply listen to theirs. Make it a safe conversation by trusting them. Power and rank are inescapable in organizations, so if you are above them in the hierarchy, make sure that you create a level space. You only want people at this stage who are genuinely excited about your vision, not people who feel pressured or who are looking for fast career advancement. They would not do justice to the spirit of the change that you are trying to create.

You can have people self-select by not attaching any strings, any consequences for refusing the invitation. If people are less excited than you anticipate or they cannot commit any sustained energy because it is not the right time for them, they should have the full freedom to say so. Your cause will be better served by them supporting it at a later stage when they are ready. Right now you only want those who are truly excited and fired up. You don't need too many of them. If you find three, four people who can commit time and effort to bring this vision about that is enough.

So, I reiterate: inviting people to join you to create an honest conversation that respects people's freedom to say no. Invite from your heart, share your vision, your dedication, and also your questions. Invite them to co-create the vision in collaboration with you and others. Remember people don't need another boss, so you need to be able to let go of the vision of your hero leadership and invite people into a vision of collective ownership of this project. If you have diligently worked on your own limiting beliefs and fears then you will be well positioned to speak a powerful and compelling invitation.

While the invitation is an important practice that I will come back to over and over, I do not want you to overthink it or make it into a big hurdle. As long as it is personal and sincere, and if it is honoring the person you invite, you don't need more.

Just invite people for coffee or lunch and talk to them openly about what you want to do and what you see possible and your sense of urgency.

Honor them, whatever they answer.

Even the people who will not join you have an important role to play. If your conversation was honoring them as the invitation should then you can count on them to support this idea when it goes out in the wider community. Ask them if they would like to be informed about the progress or if they can envision any other way of contributing and keeping in touch. Later on, they will be proud to have been involved early on and asked among the first and their support can prove very valuable.

Those who say yes are your people right now. Your next step is to invite them into a good collective conversation about what is the highest potential here. You want to share your vision with them but also allow space for them to bring in their vision, their perspectives, and their questions. *It definitely cannot be just about your dream.* I am stressing this, because if you cannot welcome collaboration then you need a totally different strategy. You cannot start a movement if there is no space for people to truly own, participate, and co-create with you.

In your start-up team, you are developing the seed of your wider movement. Just like a seed has all the D.N.A. of the forest that may one day sprout from it, just like a start-up sets the organizational culture for the company that it will become one day, your little group and its interactions need to model the kind of behaviors that you want to see in the bigger movement that it will engender.

How can you lead this little tribe on while also not bossing it around but allowing everybody to thrive and contribute? The practice that I offer for that purpose is something very dear to my heart that I have been practicing for many years, the Art of Participatory Leadership. It is a philosophy and a set of practices and tools that allow you to convene and host powerful conversations that create energy, commitment, and real results. I will talk about this practice in more detail in Chapter 6.

The Work of Your Start-Up Team

The work of the start-up is ultimately to come up with a good enough proposal, prototype it, improve it, and advocate for its implementation. Also, this team will be at heart of the movement that you will seek to build.

As you meet in the early stages, the most important work is to build the team. For that, you need a good mix of getting to know and trust each other and meaningful progress on what you set out to do.

Have good conversations about what the purpose is of the change that you are seeking to deliver. What is your common vision of what could be possible? What are your individual motivations, and what are your meaningful stories in your lives that led you here? To get to know each other so that you can create an environment of trust. At this stage, it pays not to rush. Give it some unproductive time, a couple of meetings where you share resources and inspiration. Good conversations that are not crowded out by the need to produce. If you honor this important phase you will discover skills and gifts in everybody that you will be able to use productively.

Of course, you don't want to become a talk shop, just a group of friends bouncing ideas around and dreaming together without any consequence. After the second or third meeting, you can move on to take some decisions together about your next steps. Don't go too fast or you could risk that people come into things without fully understanding each other's underlying assumptions or feel very pressured and retreat even when they could have contributed in some way but they did not have the time to find their place in the team.

A great way to build a team is to share an experience such as going to an inspiring event, learning some skills together, or attending a workshop. Such investment of time and effort demonstrates interest and commitment and give people a common experience to relate to. Besides, it can be beneficial to your project. Take time afterward to talk about it, share your insights and learnings, so it is not just an "outing," but a meaningful learning situation for your team.

The next step of your little team is to design a prototype of the solution that you are proposing (prototyping and trying out things early on is important, and I have therefore dedicated the entire Chapter 8 to prototyping). The job here is to try things out, not to come up with the perfect solution. For one, a perfect solution might just not be at all possible, but what you are also doing here is establishing a pattern of trying things out fast and failing forward, learning and improving. Nothing will give you such useful evidence about what is working and what doesn't than actually trying out your ideas. Perfect planning also doesn't exist. Establishing an entrepreneurial mindset of doing things and then learning from the results, good and bad, will give you an edge.

In this early stage, you gather information and learning. You gather case studies, examples, feedback, questions, and testimonials. Eventually, you have a much clearer picture of where chances and possibilities lie. You might have already some good solutions that you can confidently propose.

If you have gotten this far, you have planted the seeds for your success. Not only have you identified what is not working, but you are actively improving it. You have assembled your team to work on it too. You talk about it and you learn together how to make an even better solution.

Sustainability

At this stage, I want to note that sometimes (not always) this is easy to integrate with your general work volume, maybe because it is closely related to your regular work.

Sometimes it takes a significant extra investment of time and energy and sometimes your money, as you might pursue extra learning opportunities that are not fully covered by your company. This may also be true (it is probably true) for your start-up team members. This is where your and their motivation comes into play. You will need to dedicate resources for this initiative and if it is not important, it is definitely not going to happen as you proceed as a team.

What does it take to make this effort sustainable for each of you? What nourishes you? What supports you? These are questions to ask ourselves at the beginning and throughout.

What can you dedicate to this start-up and what resources are at your disposal? The more you and your colleagues can align it with your work and secure some sort of mandate, the easier it is, but in the early stages of your project, you may just need to bootstrap. Dedicate some of your spare time and personal resources. Remind yourself why you are doing it, and have a very honest conversation with your team about how to make this sustainable. You and the team will need to view this entire project with energy and enthusiasm. What does it take for you all to sustain momentum? This is a crucial conversation to have.

Above Board or Underground?

It may also be the case that you want to start your project "underground," meaning not very "officially." Some of my clients chose to do that because they were afraid that exposing their idea too soon would result in it being perceived as a threat and killed off. Depending on the context, that can be a good choice.

I am not a fan of the "top secret;" I would rather that rumor works for you and not against you. People will find out about it anyway.

Successful intrapreneurs that I have witnessed launched and tried out innovation without much fanfare, following the Nike motto: *Just do it!*

Only when they gathered enough evidence and "grassroots" support did they start to look for official recognition of what they were doing. Being "in the shadows" allowed them much more freedom for any kind of conversation and real creativity.

chapter 6

Building a Movement

nitiatives and ideas come and go in all organizations. Every day, people come up with solutions, brainstorm ideas, consult and propose new approaches, and leaders lay new tracks for the future. What is the difference between the ideas that stick and the ones that are never pursued or abandoned early? It is certainly not how good they are, as the value of many of them cannot be known in advance (and we know of many bad ideas that are pursued). What gives some ideas advantage over others is the support they get from the people who matter, the people in the organization, the leadership, the stakeholders.

If they identify with an idea or a proposal, this will have a much better chance to be seriously explored, considered, funded, and pursued. As an intrapreneur, especially one that proposes innovative thinking, your path to success will not be the one of the lonely hero whose contribution and ideas will be embraced because they are so brilliant. Rather, if you really want to turn your ideas into realities you will need to create a movement inside your organization, and possibly outside, that champions them. This chapter is about how you can do that.

Now that you have a dedicated team, do you really need to reach out to more people? Do you really need a movement? In a few cases, the small team is enough. The solution will speak for itself and it will deliver such an obvious improvement with such a low cost that your company will automatically take it on. In this case, you only need to show it to the right person responsible and it will be taken from there. If this sounds too good to be true, it is because it often is.

Many changes championed by my clients would need investment from the company and in many cases significant changes in how people behave and/or internal processes. Sometimes they would like to see improvement in organization culture, the approach to management, environmental or social awareness and responsibility, and so on. Such changes are of course possible. Organizations change and adapt all the time, but you need to have a larger group of people passionately believing in and advocating for their shared purpose in order to create certain complex and difficult transformations (especially so if the initiative does not come from the top). In most cases, except when you are championing a narrow technical solution, the work of the start-up team is also to start and support a movement of engaged users, collaborators, and participants. The next task of the start-up team is to invite engagement from other people within the company. What I call building a movement is a process of inviting and engaging in conversations that are relevant to your initiative.

Who Is in Your Movement?

The answer is simple: it's anybody who is a stakeholder. You want to create a forum for people to engage with the ideas, contribute their questions and their stories, and to make it even better. You want these people to be informed, support the initiatives and changes that you are championing. You want them to identify themselves with it and help you build a story and knowledge base that will make your proposals so much better and more functional. You want the people who connect joyfully to the vision and the ideas that you propose, and if you are really open to their contribution, the actual users can take the ideas and run with them. Improve, innovate, find ways of using them or context that you would have never thought about. Like app developers using the iPhone platform, your movement will invest itself in the proposed innovation and will bring out its real potential. You will receive that energy, excitement, and validation for your hard work above all, the impact that you can hope for will grow beyond what you can directly manage and plan for.

Start with an Invitation (Again)

So where do you even start? In some ways, the process of building a movement starts in the same way you start building your start-up team: with an invitation. However, this time you are not the only one inviting. The entire team should work together to co-create and sign the invitation so that it speaks to your stakeholders and they understand that it is special. You invite them to engage with your proposals, but from their perspective. You invite them to be part of a laboratory or playground where they can bring their creative selves and talk about aspects that are meaningful and interesting to them. A good invitation will reflect all this.

You can choose how you distribute it. In some places, you want to send it to a mailing list. In others, you might find it more appropriate to approach people individually or in small groups, even if you are thinking that the movement means many, many people, it doesn't need to be big at first. Keep it manageable and keep inviting. Once people answer your invitation and gather, make sure that the time is well spent with meaningful, authentic conversation that create value for your team and that are enriching for all the participants.

As I mentioned before, my way of making meetings work for people is a practice called Participatory Leadership.

The Art of Participatory Leadership

I could write about this practice in literally every chapter of this book because you could apply it to your first conversations with your start-up team and to any and all collaborations or meetings that you will have all along. It is more than a meeting tactic. It is a leadership path that moves the focus away from one person and onto the collective for effective collaboration toward a common purpose. This practice is also known as the Art of Hosting and Harvesting Conversations that Matter. The best way to learn about it and hit the ground running is to attend one of the three days training that you can find all over the world. I promise you they are worth it (check the references for links).

To get you started, here are some ideas:

Invite well

I have spoken already about inviting, so here I will just reiterate the need to invite well. Infuse your invitation with the spirit you want people to show up with. It is with the invitation that the gathering actually starts.

Design for a Harvest

Plan what you want the results to be clarifying and what type of new thinking you would like to take away from this meeting. How are you going to use people's contributions, their ideas, and their questions? This is a very important step because it allows you to ask the right questions and gather what you have learned in a format that is best suited for your use.

In so many meetings that I attend the usability of the meeting's outcome is an afterthought. The results are either not recorded at all or are minutes that nobody reads. I advise that you consider in advance how the outcome will be used and with whom it will be shared. That allows you to plan your harvest strategically. Examples of harvest can be action plans, checklists or just impressions, lists of resources, a purpose statement, or an invitation to the wider group. If you know what you want from the meeting, you will be able to craft better questions and plan how you want to gather the data. Maybe you need to record some snippets. Maybe you need to interview some participants in the break. Maybe you need a template, maybe you need pictures. Planning with the outcome in mind is your first step for an intentional and meaningful meeting.

Powerful Questions

Einstein once said that if you would have one hour available to solve a problem, he would take fifty-five minutes to figure out the right question. Once you have a really good question, it is much easier to figure out the answer. Powerful questions will ignite powerful conversations. If you get in the habit of spending some time during the meeting preparation finding and crafting a good question, I guarantee you that your results will be amazing. Choose a question that is a burning question for you or for the preparatory team. What is the question that if answered would make the biggest difference to your group, to your initiative?

Ask yourself: are your questions genuine? Do they reflect your genuine curiosity and create a space for people to contribute?

Also: what assumptions are we making? What are we taking for granted as we are asking these questions?

How are our assumptions limiting us? How can we make our questions even more powerful by letting go of our limiting assumptions and focusing on possibility?

Instead of asking, "How can we convince management to commit to work on an environmental project?" we can ask, "How do we effectively invite those who really care about the environmental impact?"

Or instead of asking, "How can we create a more flexible work environment, so we can work more from home?" we can ask: "What does it take for us to trust in each other so that we deliver our best work (wherever we choose to do it)?".

When you invite people in a room to a meeting, invest time in working out a powerful question. It makes a world of difference to the quality of the meeting and the outcome, and it honors the time and effort the participants are investing in it.

Create a Safe Environment

For a meaningful conversation to take place, people will need to be safe to express their real thoughts and feelings. In an organization that iş rife with competition and power games this is not to be taken for granted. But you can do it. First of all, start right at the beginning with agreements on confidentiality. What is shared in this room will stay in the room. Also by using some techniques that allow everybody space to speak without being interrupted. By starting in a circle where people speak one after another, every voice will be heard and everybody can be seen, and you can improve people's sense of safety. It is a small step with a huge impact.

Circle is an ancient and powerful meeting practice and I describe it in detail in the tools chapter of my previous book, which I offer to you for free download at www.playthe systembook.com. If you want to dig into this methodology even further, please consult the references for further reading.

If you happen to have in a meeting people with lots of formal power in the hierarchy, you have to prepare for that.

Ask them in advance to share their hearts and their own burning questions in the meeting and help establish the safe space by showing up authentically by showing humanity and vulnerability.

Of course, it is not enough to feel safe. Even more important is to *be* safe.

I recommend radical transparency about why you invite, who you invite, how you will share the harvest, and what next steps you envision.

Their participation in the movement should be a joyous and empowering experience and not a place where they feel exposed, observed, and uncomfortable.

As the host of the meeting, your job is to be fully present. Prepare a process that honors the group and the purpose and leads to a good result. Be fully present and move the process along, making sure that nobody will abuse or monopolize the space.

A safe space might sound elusive, but I can tell you with great certainty that it is possible. What makes it possible above all is that other participants are there because they answered an invitation from the heart because they care about the topic. Your job is to hold them and honor their investment throughout the meeting.

Invite Contribution and Collaboration

Depending on the size of your group and on what you want the outcome to be there are myriad of good facilitation methods that you can use to allow all the voices in the room to be heard. If you want the people to engage with the idea and create a movement, they need to be able to fully invite themselves, their ideas, and perspectives into it. That can mean that your initial idea will be challenged, debated, taken apart, and reassembled. Don't worry. This is about engagement and improvement, not design by committee. Many people are worried to invite others in because they fear that their ideas will be taken away from them or changed beyond recognition. They prefer to sell their ideas when they are ready for presentation to other people. There are a lot of limiting beliefs in this approach, so make sure that you do your inner work to be able to welcome engagement (which is, anyway, the only way to go toward sustainable change).

To learn about some of my favorite tools for meaningful conversation and collaboration, here is an extra gift for you: the chapter on tools from my previous book *The CEO's Playbook* to download for free at www.playthesystembook.com.

Allow the Not Knowing

I talked before about the importance of powerful questions. What is also special about these questions is that they don't have obvious answers. Often times they are asking for a change in perspective, a totally new way of thinking (and yet we rush to answer all the questions).

Resist this problem-solving urge. Sitting with a question is uncomfortable for many people even for a short time.

Yet if you design a good process around it then that honors and acknowledges that none of us has the answer yet. The conversation will yield new thinking, new perspectives and creative solutions, or at least the ingredients to a creative solution. Only by going beyond the usual thinking and answers can we reach to the new. Your job is to design and hold a safe and confident space for your conversation.

You as a Participatory Leader

As the initiator of your movement, you assume leadership role. You will do various things in this role. Advocate, present, develop the ideas, inspire, and create a movement. Sometimes you will host a round of creative conversations. Sometimes you want to be part of the conversation, not the host. For those situations, I absolutely advise you to get facilitation and hosting support. Mixing roles can bring confusion to the people and kill the collaborative spirit because it looks and feels like manipulation.

Get clarity first and then ask for help and support. Your start-up team colleagues might be able to offer that support. Or you might ask somebody else who has the skills to do it. Remember, clarity in your head about who you are in a particular conversation will create clarity and energy in the group. You are now set to invite and hold some of the most amazing, engaging, and creative conversations with people. If the conversations are hosted well, people will show up so excited and creative, with so much authenticity, that you will be delighted and surprised. Harvest them well, and make sure that the learning will be reflected back to the community as you are pursuing with them the changes that you dream about.

Keep It Up

One meeting is not a movement, but an ongoing series of encounters where people can engage with a topic can be the birth of a movement. You will want to commit to keep inviting and hosting such conversations over and over. Sometimes more people will come. Sometimes less. Sometimes you won't be able to be there. This is why you have a team. However, consistence is key. You need to provide for other people to keep coming back and engage with ideas and developments.

Feeding Back into the Movement

Beyond holding meetings, you as a group need to figure out how you can feed back the harvests, the impressions, into the group. You need a channel for that. It can be a newsletter, a YouTube channel, an online platform, or a mix of all these. The idea is that you reflect back to the community in some ways what came out of their investment of time and energy.

This work is also an opportunity for people in the movement to engage more with it. You don't need to (and you should not) do everything by yourself. This is an opportunity to engage people beyond your start-up team. Maybe some of them will become part of that. My message here is clear. Your movement will not happen by itself. It needs nurturing, ongoing invitation, places and opportunities to gather, forward conversations, relationships, and a place, ideally online, where people can plug into it. Of course this will not happen overnight! You will start small, but know that you can go far from there.

Chapter 7

Wisdom Circle: Sponsorship, Mentorship, and Resources

"We make a living by what we get, but we make a life by what we give."

– Winston Churchill

I am a big fan of democracy, but we both know that most organizations these days are not run as democracies but rather that power flows from the top down, like in a feudal kingdom (or an army). There are, of course, exceptions and if you work in a modern organization that grants you lots of freedom and power, congratulations. (And get in touch. I am a passionate student of these new forms of organization.) But if you, like the large majority of employees worldwide, are working in a more traditional workplace (and you are not the CEO), then you will find it useful to learn to get more power and influence your cause and your movement.

The more transformational your initiative, the more resistance it is likely to encounter. New thinking and new proposals always elicit resistance even if they make a lot of sense because they might mean change to the way people work, to the traditional authority lines in the organization. Lateral thinking can be perceived as threatening to the established authority and your early success can create a backlash.

You want to have support from some people in the higher hierarchy who can provide legitimacy to your request, support, and even protection if necessary and can help get the resources you need when you take your project to the next level. Not only that, but just like experienced investors, these people can provide you with a different and valuable perspective on the company and experience and contribute to the work just as anybody would do.

And, not least of all, if you are proposing a fundamental transformation, your only chance for ultimate success is buy-in from the leadership. Successful transformation initiatives don't always have to start at the top, they can start with you (or any other intrapreneur), but the formal leadership has to have ownership of any systemic change. This is a pre-requisite for success.

This chapter is about getting the sponsorship, mentorship, and support from the hierarchy that you need for the long-term success of your vision.

Ask for It

The reason number one people don't get support for their initiatives is that they don't seek it consistently.

People don't ask because they don't know themselves what exactly to ask for and also because they tell themselves in advance that it will be useless, a waste of time (hello, limiting beliefs!).

When you have an idea and you want to launch it in the world, as an entrepreneur does, you start by looking into what it is that you need to make your first step. As Ryan Holmes said, "When in doubt, bootstrap. Using your own personal resources is the easiest way to start a business. You don't have to convince investors about the merits of your idea. You just have to convince yourself."

What resources do you need? Some of your most important resources are your time, availability, and presence, and that one of your co-innovators. Finding the right people is crucial and that is what the entire Chapter 5 is about.

But there are other resources, too. Some of them are material resources or software, computers, material for experiments, sometimes machines, sometimes simply meeting rooms with coffee and tea, flip charts, paper, and pens. In the first phase you would simply use whatever is available to you, your personal computer, your garage, your car, and any other personal resources that you can contribute to it, including money. One of the biggest differences that I encounter between entrepreneurs and employees trying to promote and realize an innovation inside an established company is the reluctance to invest themselves in that idea.

Of course, it is understandable. There are no promised riches and fast return on investment. It's not tax deductible and it might create a dent in your budget. But it also starves the idea of starter energy and love to get it off the ground. We expect other people to believe in our ideas and invest in them. We need to model this belief and behavior. What is it that your initiative needs at the beginning? A meeting space on the weekend? Training that the company will not pay for? Cake to make a meeting nicer, more inviting, and more productive? A fee for an online course or a coach for you and the team? You might be able to afford many or at least some of the smaller things needed. I am not advocating great expense or going into debt to subsidize an innovation project for your company, but if it really matters to you, then don't get hung up on the smaller stuff. It is an investment in you, after all, and it will be ultimately your success.

Think of it as a hands-on master study, a learning journey that will give you great experiences and insights and very possibly help you fulfill some personal goals. It is a way of taking ownership of your initiative to just go ahead and do it with what you have available, even if you will have to use some personal resources. Being creative about resourcing your initiative at the beginning is an essential factor of success.

Find the Treasures around You

Many companies offer resources that intrapreneurs could use strategically: training courses, training budgets for external training or competencies, coaching offers, or mentorship schemes.

These are all valuable, especially if you can approach the training department or H.R. and ask for special training or support that you would need. If they can't offer what you need, then there is maybe a possibility that they could support your participation in a learning offer outside of the company. Mentorship schemes establish contact with more senior colleagues, who can then help you through their networks approach more senior people for support. Even when you need a specific equipment, a studio or a workshop, if you go for it and ask, it might be easier to get than you thought. Of course you have to be flexible and ask within reason, but don't make the mistake of being too shy or waiting for the moment when your initiative is 100 percent backed and supported through the official channels.

As an intrapreneur, your job is to secure the resources you need to go and create the conditions that are good enough so you can start. Doing this and thinking like an entrepreneur is what will set you apart in the world from the wannabes who know how everything could be done better, if only ever somebody would listen to them.

So ask yourself and your start-up team, what is it that we really need at this point to get started, to get experience, learn, iterate, and improve? Not what are the ideal, platinum class conditions, but the minimal conditions to get going are what you need.

Your Most Important Currency: Relationships

There is a true disconnect between some of the mental models we have about organizations and how they actually work, especially when looking at bigger institutions or companies. We learned to think about them as machines, like engines. This approach comes from the 19th century when the steam engine was the pinnacle of engineering and entire factories had to be organized so that the people fit in with the machines, served the machines—think of assembly lines—and not the other way around. The more people were like machines, the thinking went, the more efficient and productive everything would be.

We can see how seductive this thinking is and of course there is a valid point. Robotic lines are unmatched in efficiency, but people are not robots and the mechanistic view has failed in addressing human dynamics and organization. The organizational chart that describes the reporting lines but that does not start to describe the multitude of relationships, good and fraught, that exist in an organization. And just like through an electric grid the energy and the information, the life force of every organization, travels not only through the line described on the chart, but to all the other lines too, complementing and sometimes replacing the official channels.

This is not bad. It simply is so. A failure to recognize how people function (as opposed to machines) has led to simplistic views and unrealistic expectations. Recognizing it helps us navigate these complex and interconnected systems.

For you as an intrapreneur, this is good news. It means that you can get essential support from people in your company and you are not limited to what the organization chart says. You can in principle, talk to anybody about anything. The organizational chart describes the hierarchy or form of power represented physically by titles, corner offices, secretaries, pay gaps, and other markers. The informal power is much more nimble. It has no form or manifestation but can move mountains, too.

Some people have an amazing ability to connect with others, we call them super connectors. They seem to know everybody and have all the inside intelligence. You find them in all kinds of positions, but often they are the secretaries and they have extensive networks and seemingly access to everybody. Most of us are not that way, but we still have quite significant networks that span departments, functions, and hierarchy. Cultivating your relationships in your organization is the most important thing you can do to advance your initiatives and also your career.

I don't recommend strenuously faking interest to try to get into the good graces of higher-ups. Rather I contend that if you cultivate genuine interest in people, you will find that everybody is relatable and everybody will have one story at least that you can deeply connect to.

You will only get this connection if you are open to it. If you expose yourself to opportunities and learn to listen deeply. If you listen to understand and to connect, you honor people. One thing that keeps us back from expanding our networks beyond people who are very similar to us is an "us" versus "them" attitude. That applies to people who work in different jobs, different organizations, and people who are below or above us in the hierarchy.

But if you abolish this limiting belief, you open yourself to connection and support from people you would have not expected. You can grow and cultivate your network by answering yes to invitations, showing up for them when they need it, putting yourself in situations of storytelling, sharing, and listening. Think about them, their passions, and their needs. How can you support them? A good word, an interested question. The simple act of witnessing them and acknowledging them. If they invite you to something that is important to them and their work, share it, support it, and show up if you can. Connecting is the opposite of ignoring.

Show up consistently in networks that discuss ideas connected to what you want to create or change. Listen and contribute. Get to know the people. This is not rocket science, yet it is often neglected. The efficiency focus our culture has does not value relationships, and building them is not on almost anybody's job description and when it is, it's for lobbyists. It feels almost creepy because it is not about genuine human connection but is purely transactional.

Being an active and caring part of your workplace community will benefit every aspect of your work life, including your initiatives. It builds up your social capital that is among your highest assets. When you need a certain type of support, make sure you define exactly what you need and then turn to your community and network for support. If you have a clear idea about what support you need and a good network, you have a greater chance to get help. More than that, people will feel involved in your project already because they supported you and by doing that, they now have a stake in your success.

Asking for help and support is not a sign of weakness, as many people seem to believe, but a sign of trust and openness; it is a kind invitation to witness your work and to participate in it.

Social Influence: How to Get through Other People's Limiting Beliefs

When you are looking for support you are inviting commitment. You want people to show up in the service of the purpose that you are hopefully sharing.

Yet very often people won't commit, and even if they do they won't keep the commitments. That will mostly say something about their limiting beliefs. If you pay attention and you understand the real reasons they don't react as you (and they) would like, you can use a number of strategies to help them overcome their own hurdles.

The reasons for them not to act, even if it would make more sense, fall generally in four big categories:

1. They don't really agree with the idea.
2. They are worried about what other people will think and say about them.
3. They don't believe they have the ability to do what is expected of them (perform the task).
4. They have a hard time translating their intention into behavior.

Depending on what is behind their reason you need a different strategy to make them act.

1. **If they don't believe it is a good idea**

This is the only case when presenting more arguments, more evidence might make people change their position.

Make your best case, present the facts, the evidence, the success stories. Talk about the consequences of action, and also of inaction. If you know your audience, you will know what matters to them, and you can highlight those consequences accordingly.

Of course, there is no guarantee that people will change their minds. Everybody is entitled to their point of view, and to their limiting beliefs. But they might.

The more examples you can use, the better it is. When you face a skeptical audience, it pays to preempt the objections and the counterarguments that you might get. Include their objections and your answers to them in your presentation.

2. **Social Factors**

When people are worried about what other people think or say about them, you would not help them by giving them more facts and arguments.

If they believe, for example, that a more self-organized and less controlled management approach would be a good idea, but they think that other managers look down on such an approach and judge it as not serious enough, then you can help them by either emphasizing or de-emphasizing what others might think.

If you have evidence that other managers also support a self-organized, participatory approach (or maybe even implement it), you can use those examples to ease the worry.

If on the other hand there are indeed no such examples that you know of, you can point to examples from other organizations and underline the pioneering, role modeling aspect of supporting such an innovative approach.

3. **Perceived lack of ability**

Sometimes, people would like to do something that they see as aligned with their values or where they see benefits but they don't believe that they have the ability to do so.

They may think that they don't have the time or they don't have the skills. In this case, there are three strategies that you can use:

- Directly help by removing obstacles. These obstacles can be informational or substantive and you can help them either by providing them with the necessary information, or by thinking about ways to make it easy for the people to do what you would like them to do.
- Provide opportunities to experience, rehearse, and model the behavior. The experience of actually doing it will give them the confidence that they can do it again.
- Expose them to other people who show up and behave the way you would like them to behave.

4. **Converting Intentions to Actions**

Finally, if they believe it is the right thing to do and they have the ability to do it, but they are still not doing it, they might have a hard time converting their intentions to actions.

In these situations sometimes prompts and reminders might work (meeting reminders are a great example, especially when meetings are voluntary and compete with other priorities).

In other cases explicit planning, clear next steps, to do lists, and commitments might support people putting new ideas into action. When you are approaching people for support in any capacity, it pays to understand exactly how can you support them in your turn so they can effectively support you in your initiative.

The Wisdom Council

Depending on the nature of what your initiative or project is, you might need support from high places. This is especially so if it involves, as we have discussed in the previous chapter, creating a growing movement. The more people invest their time, the more people will want to implement and try something out of the ordinary, they will feel safer if people with authority in the company have their back. Any kind of transformation and innovation will be immeasurably likelier to be implemented or even piloted if it is also championed by people in the system who have formal authority.

We discussed some pages ago how you can get to them. It's no silver bullet, but it's the only thing that consistently works: meeting them like people and building relationships with them just as you would with anybody. Look for common stories, experiences and passions. Listen deeply and witness, support, and help them when you can.

Of course, it does not have to be only your contacts and relationships. You are a part of a team, the start-up team, and you might even have started your movement or you might be part of a movement or a community. All these people have trusted networks of their own and together you can count on the fact that you will have enough access to the leadership where you can ask for support. But what exactly are you asking for?

If your project is ongoing or it has a longer development phase or longer implementation phase, it needs ongoing support. Take the example of a governmental organization that I am advising. My client's team wanted to create a self-organized community of practice for the middle managers, a pretty large endeavor as they had over 1,000 of them. While there was a lot of excitement among the target group, this project also needed acknowledgment so that the participants could free up some time to meet and talk about common issues and exchange experiences on how to deal with them. Many people felt reluctant to meet on a regular basis and participate in such an endeavor if they had to do it secretly without the backing of their bosses.

I advised the project initiators to reach out and invite four or five director level managers, maybe even one or two political appointees to act as a direct support for this community of practice. I called it the Wisdom Council. The role of the Wisdom Council is to act as a high-level advisor and a guardian to the project, in this example to the community of practice. The members of the Wisdom Council will understand fully the endeavor, they will identify with its purpose and will support it. They will not participate in the minutiae of the project, but they will meet from time to time to talk (maybe once a quarter) about the progress on a high level in a more strategic sense. This particular project did not need extra resources. They had enough to implement and support the first stages of this community. The job of the Wisdom Council was to provide high level legitimacy, to act as ambassadors for the importance of it.

If this is the kind of support you need for your project, I advise you to invite your senior supporters to a Wisdom Council. This gives them a position, a standing role and honors them in their special contribution. Of course, this is another piece of work for you, the start-up team.

A Wisdom Council starts with a scouting phase, when you identify who would be the right people to invite. Find people who have shown interest and demonstrate commitment to the same topics that you are seeking support for. Your work can contribute to their larger vision and to their legacy and that can be a very powerful driver.

Then the next phase is the invitation. I have talked extensively already about invitation in previous chapters and this is no different. You need to pay attention and invite them, honoring them in the process. You will have to share the purpose and the scope of your project, connect them with your vision and hopes for it.

Shortly after they have agreed, find a good date and invite them all for the first Wisdom Council meeting. These are not operational meetings. You will provide high level updates and ask for advice on the kinds of topics where they really can help. In the example mentioned, a good question for the Wisdom Council is: "How do we communicate with the directors in all departments about the value and importance of this community?" But the role of the meetings of the Wisdom Council is to make it stronger by strengthening the relationships between the senior leaders. They will know each other's commitment to this topic and by witnessing each other, their own commitment and contributions tend to grow.

The Wisdom Council needs nurturing and that is also part of the work of the start-up team. They will need ongoing high-level updates, invitations to relevant events, and the regular but not frequent meetings. Keep yourself accountable to them. Show how you have incorporated their support and advice in the work. They need to be treated with honor and acknowledged, just like a board of directors would want to be treated.

You can, of course, decide to also invite people external to the company to your Wisdom Council if appropriate. You can have industry experts or other people of high standing that can support your cause, but this is highly context dependent. Some organizations or companies cannot stand to be advised from outside and such support would create backlash rather than help.

Connect to the Bigger Movement

Your initiative or project might be unique and innovative in the company. But there are good chances that something similar or related is already happening elsewhere. The change that you are championing will be part of the bigger movement. Indeed, you might have been inspired by the bigger movement in the first place. If you connect to it not sporadically but on a regular basis, it will have many benefits for you and your initiative and movement.

- **Relationships:** By forging relationships in this community you can call upon them without hesitation when you have a particularly sticky question. You will also be seen and recognized as a member of the community.
- **Strength:** Bring your start-up team and/or movement in touch with the larger movement. Being part of something bigger offers legitimacy and it is very empowering. People here understand what you are trying to do and chances are they also have their own story of struggle and success to share. You make the larger movement even larger and stronger by showing up and the movement makes you stronger.
- **Resources:** Meeting with peers from outside the organization is an amazing opportunity to share resources and case studies. These resources can be experienced and they can be sources of financing and so on. Add your knowledge and experience generously and profit off of the learning of the larger community.

Get Yourself out of the Box

Last but not least, I want to mention a very valuable and powerful resource, an outside perspective or a fresh new approach. Often when you are blocked on something, you need to approach the problem from a new perspective and you will see possibilities that you didn't knew existed. Putting yourself in a new perspective with a creative mindset is a valuable resource. However, we often don't plan for this strategy. If anything, this happens by accident. I advise you to plan it. Bring your team and your project to outside events and ask for input and perspective on it or parts of it from total strangers. Even once in a while, this is where the goal, the new solutions will come from.

In this day and age, we have access to so much knowledge and information. You can learn about most things online for free or almost free. But having an Aha moment, a new perspective or insight will not come from linear thinking, but rather something radically unexpected. And it can lead to a quantum leap in places where you are stuck before.

So, where to go? The possibilities are endless. It could be outside workshops, conferences, or hackathons. It could be festivals for film or music or art. It can even be silent meditation in a monastery for some days. Give up a narrow expectation of what you think a solution to your dilemma or problem needs to be and you open yourself to a creative approach in solving it. Your solution or quantum leap can come in many forms, a powerful question, a new tool, a new contact that you meet, a new book that you are recommended, or it could simply be from you seeing the situation in a new light. The world around us is abundant in resources, but we are often unable to access most of them because we can't see them as resources that are available for us to take.

chapter 8

Prototype

"I have not failed. I've just found 10,000 ways that won't work."

— Thomas Edison

As the initiator of change, of an innovation, the future has already arrived in your mind. You are the holder of the vision and the potential of what is possible together with your start-up team.

On the ground, however, your idea needs to grow legs and gain traction, as well as improve into the best version of itself.

Trying your ideas out in early stages will allow you to learn, get feedback, improve, and build your movement in the same time.

If the idea of trying out, experimenting and failing sounds scary: I hear you!

In many companies and organizations, learning and failing forward are two of the buzzwords coming from the fast-moving world of tech start-ups. But buzz is all there is to it.

In reality, many established companies have created a culture of risk reduction, and intolerance to the unknown and to making any mistakes. Yet innovation is by definition creating something new, and the expectation to get it right and to have all the answers to all the questions right from the beginning is unrealistic.

If you start from a position of not much power and no mandate you might feel the pressure to have all the answers and present the perfect solution right from the beginning. But don't give in to this thought. It is a dangerous limiting belief.

Starting early and starting small, making most of the mistakes early, and learning how to mitigate them incorporating feedback from early users and practitioners is actually the least risky strategy with the highest chances for success.

A Playful Mindset

If you have the opportunity to observe children playing and building with LEGO blocks, you will see the prototyping mindset at work. They are focused, and relaxed. They try various parts, change, experiment. When it breaks down, they will observe what went wrong and try to improve on that part of the design. If it works fine they will play with it, try it out, and enhance it further. Mostly they have fun. They always start over, keep trying, and improve on their design. When they are stuck, they ask for help.

This relaxed, engaged, focused, and playful approach is what allows them to keep going, and keep learning and creating even better performing designs.

In bringing your initiative forward, you need to emulate this playful spirit.

I realize that this is easier said than done, given how foreign the concept of play is for most corporate environments. Maybe you are under intense pressure to make something happen, and playful feels flippant or even dangerous. It's also counter intuitive. You want to create something new *and* great—fast. Here is the big secret to why so many such initiatives fail: the chances of doing this without certain ease, without an open mind for trial and error is almost non-existent.

So, just try to take a little time to have some fun with your team as you design your prototype.

Depending on what your project is, a prototype may well be an action, an activity. Or, it could be a simplified version, maybe just one feature of what your final outcome would be.

For example, if you want to implement self-organization, you could start by experimenting with collaborative agenda setting (agile meetings) or try out consent-based decision making in a couple of instances (these are features and practices of self-organized companies and organizations).

Whatever it is, take some of the features that you want to test and find easy ways to try them out and get feedback.

Designing

There are many ways to build and plan prototypes. There are entire disciplines, such as Design Thinking, or Human Centered Design, that help you create prototypes in an interactive and relevant way. If you are familiar with these approaches, please use them for approaching your project planning. They are amazing for helping you design your project, and ultimately your product, and interventions.

In the following pages I will introduce you to another approach, one that I have successfully used with many people. It is based on (and a modified version of) a methodology called "Design for Wiser Action," that was developed by the Art of Hosting community, my professional community.

This methodology consists of a template and a process. The template (that I call the canvas) might look, at first sight, like a normal project planning tool, and indeed, it is something like that. Yet, it has some significant differences. It guides you through a number of important questions that you and your team can answer together. It focuses you on the conversations you need to have so you can create meaningful action leading to the results that you seek.

Prototypes are also included in this canvas, so you can approach them deliberately and systematically. Here is how to use it.

The Process

The canvas gives you the basis for conversation, the prompts, and the place to gather your answers. It is a visual tool that you can find in this chapter, or you can download a larger version of it suited for print at www.playthesystembook.com

This work is primarily the work of the start-up team, with input from other people, too.

Print or draw the canvas as big as you can. Ideally as big as a flip chart paper, and gather around it with pens and Post-Its. This work is not only giving you information, but having these conversations and coming up together with answers creates cohesion and alignment in your team, so make sure that you take a couple of hours, and fill out the answers together. I recommend that you use Post-Its. Write on them first and not directly on the canvas. That will give you the freedom to be spontaneous, add and change easily.

Once you are through, the next step in the process is to get feedback. Invite in a group of your potential partners, Wisdom Council, and stakeholders, and explain it to them. Then ask for their feedback and thoughts. In this phase, the best you can do is listen. You don't yet want to convince them about anything, just sit there and take note of their comments, feedback, and critiques. Don't argue, just listen (the less you speak in this meeting, the better). Don't forget to thank them in the end.

If it is hard to organize all these people to come together (you don't need more than five), then you can also take it to them individually, although the group setting has distinct advantages. By being in a group it allows your consultants to have a creative conversation that can be very helpful to you. So, just write down the feedback, ask for clarification if needed. Then bring back the feedback to your team. The new perspectives will be valuable building blocks, and will give you good information to integrate in your canvas.

You might not take everything on the board, but everything's the basis for a good conversation.

If you approach this seriously, and as a team, you will have a good basis for how to proceed. It will give you clarity about what you are proposing, what and how you are prototyping, about the resources you have, the ones you need, and about your timeline. It will help you approach people for your Wisdom Council and create an invitation for your movement. Of course, this is still a draft. You will not have the absolute final version until it is literally over, and your project is completed. You want to be able to plan but also adapt and learn, to create the best and most viable version of the change that you want to bring into the world.

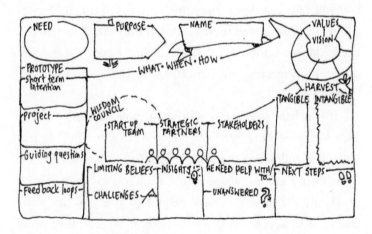

The Canvas

Here are some short explanations for the spaces that you need to fill in on the canvas.

Need

> *"If we tried to think of a good idea we wouldn't have been able to think of a good idea. You just have to find a solution for a problem in your life."*
> – **Brian Chesky**, Co-founder of AirBnB

This is the place to start. When you started thinking of your initiative or of your project, you probably answered the need that you observed or a need that you had. Describe this need in the words of your beneficiaries, of your stakeholders (and you might be among them). If you can clearly define what problem you are solving and what need in the world you are planning to meet, your team and stakeholders will have a much easier time knowing if you are on the right path and if there is something in it for them or not. If you meet a real need, one perceived by many people, it will be easy to invite sponsors to support you.

Examples of needs are: need for affordable housing, need for knowledge sharing, collaboration, need for faster, more efficient and wiser decision making, need to reduce waste, etc.

Purpose

The purpose of your project or initiative is the most important part of this chart. It is where you formulate your raison d'être, your reason for pursuing this change, and your intention with it. If you get your purpose right, and you never lose sight of it, you will have an easy time talking about it and sharing your idea with other people. Also you will intuitively always know what is yours to do for this project and what is not. A clear purpose is an easy test. Whatever aligns with it can be considered as a worthy action, and whatever doesn't align with it is not for you to pursue.

You might also think that writing a purpose (or mission statement) is only something for big organizations or corporations (and you might also think it is only empty words, as they sometimes are). But it does not have to be like this. Your purpose can be one of your most powerful instruments, and writing it will bring you, your team, and all who engage with your project, clarity and agency.

So how to create a good mission statement that clarifies your purpose? A good way is to draft a statement that answers these three questions.

1. **What do you want to do?**

What is your initiative or project doing? What is your gift to your beneficiaries? Here you want to be as specific as possible. It might be "create a network," "create a community of practice," "introduce self-organized teams," "put the issue of oceans governance high on the agenda of the European Union, in the light of climate change," or "create flexible and better working conditions for employees." Whatever it is that you propose to do, whether it's a thing like to building a new app or creating an organizational process, be specific about it and fully own it.

2. **How do you do it?**

This is about your values, what is important. As you pursue your goals, what values are guiding you in your work and inform your worldview? Examples of values are: participation, knowledge sharing, voluntarism, access, equality, efficiency, sustainability, and affordability. Whatever is important to you. Expand your "what" with the "how."

The "create a network" will be "create knowledge sharing, engaging network of practitioners." "Put the issue of oceans governance high of the agenda of European Union" will be "Put the issue of oceans governance high of the agenda of European Union by engaging the stakeholders in the European Commission."

3. **Why do you do it? To what end?**

This is the most important part because it gives meaning to the entire initiative.

You can do that easily by adding "so that" after the first two points and then add your why. Our examples would then look like this: "Create an engaging community of practice so that your practitioners in all departments have access to support and information and can together continuously improve their field of expertise." Or: "Put the issue of oceans governance high on the agenda of the European Union by engaging all the relevant stakeholders in the European Commission so that they can take decisive action to protect the ecosystem."

You have the content at this point. If you feel inspired and crafty, you can play around with formulation, simplify, and streamline.

Vision

On the other side of the canvas there is a space to write your vision. This is your high-level hope and image of the future that you would like to see. How would you like this work to impact the world? How would you like this to impact the company, your stakeholders, in ten or fifteen years? Think even further beyond. What is the highest potential of this work? The need and the vision are bookending this process. You will be working from what you see right now, toward what you want to see and create.

Principles

Our principles, which we can also call our values, tell us what is important to us. They will be evident in our vision, in our purpose, and how we decide to tackle the need that we see. Expressing them is a useful exercise. A lot of it we take for granted but taking time to collectively clarify in our team what are very specifically the common principles that underpin this project will create alignment.

This is also a team building process: talking about what is important to each of you and sharing examples of these principles at work will bring you closer together. Also, you will have a clear guidance about what are good ways to pursue your goal and who the people are who can help you, people who are aligned and in sync with your values.

Harvest

I also call this the results. Harvest is a word that comes from agriculture. It represents the results of what we plant and cultivate: the results of efforts. This is an essential part of our canvas, as we want to have clarity in advance about what we want our results to be. We can plan towards achieving them. We differentiate between tangible harvest and intangible harvest.

Tangible harvests are things, like documents, reports, and artifacts. They can be qualifications, certifications, ratifying documents, and decisions. They can be any physical thing that we want to develop: a new technology, an app, or a piece of equipment. We will write in the planned harvest not only the things but the tangible measurable results that we want to see at the end of our project.

Intangible harvests are the results that are just as important, but not so easy to measure. Such intangible harvests can be: better engagement, motivation, increased participation, confidence, or stakeholder satisfaction. Very often these results are the primary results, better knowledge sharing or higher engagement are not so easy to measure directly, but they have great impact on your company or organization.

Pay great attention to this. If you are just going for tangible harvests you will have a much more difficult time to engage a movement, and even find sponsors. People want to identify with your initiative and this is an emotional attachment. So you need to reflect on how you want them to feel. What ideas should they share if they participate in or benefit from your proposal? Be sure that you think of the harvest before you decide what actions to take. You should only plan actions last, once you have enough information on what your harvest outcome should be. And lots of other information so that you can make sure that the action will deliver the result that you desire.

The next part you want to deal with by focusing on the people who are involved.

Start-Up Team

This is pretty straight forward. At this stage, if you already have your start-up team, write your names in there. If you don't have all the people yet, it is a good opportunity to brainstorm on who these people can be and how to start a conversation with them. As I mentioned before, having a team will increase the chances of your success many fold. Even if it takes effort and intention to collaborate well.

Strategic Partners

This is information that is important to your project and your movement. Who are other people outside the start-up team who support you? They can come from within your organization or from outside.

Stakeholders

You can put in this category anybody who has a stake in your project. They might be people from your company who take an interest in the project, but also beneficiaries, other actors in the field, and other groups of people who tend to be impacted by your work. You can do an entire exercise in mapping out your stakeholders. It is useful because these people are those who can be part of your movement, support you, and spread the word. Also, the clearer the picture you have about who they are and how they're impacted, the easier it will be to invite them into a conversation or even just to present your business case for sponsors and leadership. Ultimately all this information will help you plan a more relevant and impactful approach to your project.

Wisdom Council

I have described in detail in previous chapters who the people in the Wisdom Council are and what their role is. They have an important role to play and they have their dedicated place on your canvas.

Prototyping

Now it is the time to turn your attention toward designing your prototype, or prototypes, in the canvas. You have four questions that deal with that.

- What do you wish to learn in the next three to six months? What is your short-term intention?
- What will the experiment look like? (Project description.)
- What questions are you exploring with your prototype? (Guiding questions.)
- And how will you, and how often will you, harvest learning from your prototyping process? (Learning feedback and loops.)

Note that these questions focus on learning and experimentation. They guide you to try things out, starting small with a learner's mind. Gather feedback and improve your plans accordingly. You can conduct your experiments, your trial balance, with a small group of people on a small scale. The idea is to get going, start fast, and learn from it. Often with prototypes it is just the way things function. For example, when you invite your first sponsor into the Wisdom Council it is a small-scale trial. Your experiment with your invitation, with explaining your vision, your project, and their role.

It is precisely when it does not go according to plan, that a learner's mind or a playful approach is the most important, some of my clients will tell me about how discouraged they feel in such a case. They will try, but after taking note of the first rejection they will conclude that this experiment and the entire project is a failure. And feel rejected. They will the toy with the idea of giving up and maybe even quitting their job. Approaching these experiments, these prototypes, with openness and courage for mistakes is what will make them successful. Not because they worked as planned, but because you will have learned so much by doing them. No books or training can teach you more or give you more actual data about how to proceed than trying out and doing stuff.

The bottom part of the canvas looks at some further aspects of your project. It points you to think about your limiting beliefs, challenges, and resources. These questions help you look inside as well as assess your environment. Reflecting on your resources will help you see all the big and small things you have available, some of which you might have even taken for granted. Some of these resources you can even use as currency to get other resources you need and you currently don't have. For example: "If we help facilitate your activity—one of our start-up members is a trained facilitators—will you let us use your big meeting room for our event?"

Only after you have concluded all this will you plan your action. The reason to do this last is that by now you know so much more. You're clear about the needs that you are addressing. You have a clear purpose. You know exactly what change you are envisioning, what tangible and intangible outcomes you want to harvest. You know your team, your Wisdom Council, your purpose, and your stakeholders. You have analyzed your environment, challenges, and resources. Now you can make the preliminary plan of your actions. I say preliminary because you will as a matter of course adapt the plans after each trial and prototype. But to start with, this is the moment to lay out your actions, what, how, and when. You can draft your actions before or after you decide on your prototypes. But either way what you learn from the prototypes should be taken into consideration in all your actions.

chapter 9

Tell your story;
Change the Culture

Some organizations are like tribes or villages, and some of them are like big cities. There are many people living there, and they have clear rules about how things work. They also have a predominant overview that will codify a lot of what is possible or likely, even if it's not written down in detail anywhere. This is the organizational culture (or worldview), a set of stories, and beliefs. If you found it hard to pursue your passion and innovation, it probably will be because "things work differently around here," or "we don't do such things," "we work in different ways," "that is not important," or "that is not serious".

Most of the arguments in people's minds about the system refer not to hard facts, such as the technology to do what you propose has not yet been invented, but rather are cultural. The cultural body of the organization is the sharing of stories and beliefs about what we do, how we do it, what is possible, how people are, how employees are, why do they work, and so on. This culture is both hard to change and is constantly changing.

The chapter is about helping you to shape the narrative, the culture in your organization, so that your initiative and other innovations will be embraced. Ultimately, this is going to decide the long-term viability of the change that you are seeking; if something should be done or not is not an exact science, it becomes reality and fact because enough people in the organization believe in them. If you can change the story, you can change the system. So ask yourself the question, what is the story that you want to see alive in your system, in your organization? What possible story of values , if it were to be believed by most people, would be nourishing and life giving to everybody, including to your initiative? What story of priorities, what story of courage is it?

Note how I use the word "story." Sometimes people use "story" as an antonym, as an opposite to "reality." This is not how I use it. When we talk about culture, some stories are the reality, what we consider true and worthwhile and important. Stories that we widely share with others will shape our actions and interactions as if they were some natural laws.

An example I use is the place of women in society. Which has changed and evolved a lot over the history. Nothing changed in the biology of women or men, but the stories that we tell about this biology and the impact of it are the ones that shape our lives. They empower or hinder, they result in laws, regulations, and protections to uphold them. In the way I use the term here, story is the fundamental element of our shared culture.

Find the Seeds

Whatever is the value or principle that you would like to see embodied in your organization, I am pretty sure that you can find it already in your system right now. For one, if you are on the journey yourself, you will find it in your own actions and your own values. Since you and your colleagues are part of the system, there is no denying that what you want to see more of is already there and I bet that you are not alone. While you might be an innovator, you will find the seed many places. What you need to do is find these seeds, nurture them, and build on them. This is a storytelling exercise and it can be an important part of your work in any case but especially if you are seeking culture change or system change.

But how do you find those seeds?

I suggest that you make it a central part of your activity while inviting people from your movement to meet. The methodology that I recommend to use is called Appreciative Inquiry. I have described this method in my previous book and you can download this and the entire tools chapter at www. playthesystembook.com. Also you can study this approach extensively and in-depth and you will find further reading about it in the references. In these pages I will just describe the essence of this approach and why I think it is the most powerful way to change the culture in ways that support your work.

The core belief of Appreciative Inquiry is that bringing of our attention to something, a story, an action, a trait, that will grow and strengthen it.

An often-told parable attributed to the evangelical minister Billy Graham that illustrates this point talks about an old grandfather who is teaching his grandson about life: "A fight is going on inside me," he said to the boy. "It is a terrible fight and this is between two wolves. One is evil. He's anger, envy, sorrow, regret, greed, arrogance, self-pity, guilt, resentment, inferiority, lies, false pride, superiority, and ego." He continued, "The other one is good. He's joy, peace, love, hope, serenity, humility, kindness, perseverance, empathy, generosity, truth, compassion, and faith. The same fight is going on inside you and inside every other person too."

The grandson thought about it for a minute and then asked his grandfather, "Which wolf will win?" The grandfather simply replied, "The one you feed."

Just as in the story, the traits you pay attention to in an organization are the ones will become stronger and will even become prevalent. Paying attention to them gives them energy and makes them flourish.

So, look for those seeds.

A great exercise to build trust and community and to find what is already there is to divide people in groups of three and ask them to take turns in telling stories. Everybody will have a story. Pick one of your values, principles, and invite them. Tell the story of a situation when this value was demonstrated in your work. For example, tell a story from your work when you have worked in autonomy and you felt that you could use all your creativity. Or tell about the time when you successfully brought awareness at work to an issue that mattered to you.

In your case, you can share a story around the values or the practices that you would like to see more of in your company. Invite the two people to listen deeply and attentively and take notes about how such a success is possible. What were the enabling factors? This little activity is only the first step of an Appreciative Inquiry process. That process is much deeper and can work wonders in an organization. If you can, then by all means do it.

But even if you don't plan to go for an extended process, you can already profit a lot by just inviting people to share their stories. Already this small exercise accomplishes a number of things that are very valuable.

1. **It surfaces stories, experiences of possibility, and strength.**

You, and all who listen, will see what already exists and what already is working in your organization that is aligned with what you want to do. The stories are like gems for you, because they show you where people are ready to pursue the change that you would also like to see.

2. **It honors and strengthens people.**

The simple act of witnessing people as they share their stories of success is very powerful. We are giving the highest honor, our undivided attention and deep listening, and even if this only for fifteen minutes, the storytellers are empowered and strengthened for having shared their stories and having been witnessed.

3. **It builds community.**

As a result of the storytelling, people feel much closer to each other. For a moment, they were a part of each other's story. They learned new things about each other, some things they have not expected. Storytelling builds community.

4. **Knowledge sharing.**

By sharing stories of overcoming adversity, people will tell about their strategies and learning. This is a valuable learning methodology. Make sure that beyond your creating a good environment for a valuable storytelling session, you also prepare well for documenting the stories where you believe that seeds for the new culture are present.

Nurture the Seedlings

You can make this culture grow by bringing visibility and attention to it and what it can accomplish. Here you also use principle of the Appreciative Inquiry. What you bring your attention to, that will grow. There are many ways to do that.

You create opportunities for people to know each other and share. As I have previously mentioned, the sheer act of witnessing and being witnessed is strengthening. Such opportunities can be at meetings of your movement, but actually any situation in the organization when you can add a sub-gathering to talk about where you see signs and possibilities that your culture is expanding will work. For example, you might talk about where you are seeing participation expanding in your organization. Make sure that you document the outcomes and make them somehow visible to the participants and even beyond, if possible.

Another question for your gathering is how can we showcase and share our stories further? The people in the group will, together, be as a matter of course much more resourceful and creative than any one person can be. They will have experience and ideas about how to share elements of their stories with the wider organization.

Case Studies

Showcasing success stories is a way to honor and strengthen the particular elements of the culture that you are focusing on. This can be a great storytelling project, where people share their stories with the wider public. It can be as a storytelling session at events, or as a blog post, or as an article in the internal newsletter. Make sure that, if it is a short article, people who are interested can follow-up with some in-depth materials, such as a longer video interview about the case, or a video storytelling session either in person or virtually. I underline this because short articles or vignettes can communicate in-depth the experience and leave people who feel intrigued and inspired by the story with many, many questions still. Having a follow-up session with the case owner that can be recorded for future use is a great way to bring people along and give texture and life to the story. It is an opportunity to share detailed strategies, lessons learned, and to answer questions.

Story Harvesting Sessions

These are also versions of case studies and they are focused on learning from a particular story and experience of the storyteller. When you find some amazing cases, full of rich learning and inspiration for others, not just success, there is plenty of learning in trying and failing too. You can illuminate them and use them for interested people in the organization to learn from them. Such a storytelling and learning session can be part of a bigger event, but can also stand on its own. There is a beautiful methodology for it developed and described by Mary Alice Arthur called Collective Story Harvesting. You can consult the methodology online (see the tools chapter and in the references). It is simple and powerful and full with learning for the community and organization.

For many of the methods I describe here, I do recommend getting support from an experienced facilitator who knows these methods, or if you are so inclined, invest three days and get trained in them. You and your colleagues will not regret it. You will find a course near you at the Art of Hosting website.

While the methods look simple and easy, there is a lot of depth to them and having them facilitated by somebody who knows what they are doing will ensure that you will make the best of this occasion and reach your goal of powerfully strengthening and nurturing the culture that you want to see growing.

Connect with the Larger Cultural Trend

Your culture will be strengthened by highlighting and sharing stories from other companies from all around the world in addition to the internal stories. People will strengthen and legitimatize their behavior and values if they see that they are not alone but are part of a bigger trend. If they can see themselves as pioneers in bringing new things to their company, that strengthens them and encourages them to be even more open about their wishes and experiences.

Chapter 10

Potholes, Stumbling Blocks, and How to Navigate Them Well

So, here you have it.

Each step that I outlined is eminently doable and consists of showing up, taking responsibility, inviting people, and having meaningful conversations with them. These are steps of leadership, because whether you have an official title and mandate or not, leadership is something that you can do. All the methodologies described are successfully used by many, many people from all walks of life, and all around the world.

You have also references for further learning, and tools at your disposal.

Yet, experience shows that just knowing the steps is not enough. Most people, even as they say they really, really want to make a change, will not follow-up with action. The reason is that getting over your resistance, your internal resistance, and limiting stories, as well as persevering and staying on the course for the long haul, requires dedication and stamina.

Things don't go as planned, team members change and drop off, sponsorship requests fall on deaf ears, your direct boss opposes your ideas, and unexpected new projects and workloads land on your desk. You will find that it absolutely makes sense to give up. There are a million good reasons not to persevere, after all, you have no guarantee that you will succeed. The surge of energy and enthusiasm that you have at the beginning wears off in the face of organizational indifference. But I am not writing this to indulge a defeatist attitude, I am here to tell you that you can make a difference, and you should not waste your life by playing small. I believe in you, and I know that you need support.

In all of this work, having a support system that stands behind you will determine your success. In the later stages of the project you will start getting a lot of energy and support back. Your start-up team, the movement, the sponsors, will all reflect back to you many times over the energy and enthusiasm that you invest. But not at the beginning, right when you start you have to build your initial support system on your own. Who are they? Who are the people who listen to you, understand you, and help you focus, think, and act? Who are the people who will have your back?

I can tell you, based on my longstanding experience, that coaching helps. Get yourself a coach who understands and supports what you want to do, and you will find it an invaluable support. Instead of getting stuck every step of the way and taking lots of time and energy to unstuck yourself, you will have a structure and a form to get over your roadblocks and limitations. You will have the needed support to step up bravely and boldly, and make your mark on your organization. Maybe your organization has a scheme that can afford this support for you, if you have one use it. If you don't have, but need one, then get one anyway.

Support is always available, you just need to reach for it. I have given you many resources, some of them described in the book, some of them described in my previous book (download the tools chapter free at www.playthesystembook.com). There are many additional resources for you there.

You have everything you need to start right away, and I hope to get a glimpse of your work in the world. The world is a better place because you decided to shine your light and make a difference.

Acknowledgments

This book had many midwives. I am filled with gratitude for how much help and support I received from so many people. Without you, I couldn't do it.

First and foremost, I am grateful for the inspiration and challenge that I get from my clients. Your questions, stories and journeys keep me engaged and committed to give the best I can, every day.

I wrote this book in an attempt to answer questions that came directly from some of you, and I thank you for that!

I am thankful for my professional community, the Art of Hosting Community, for the continuous, rich path of learning and co-creation, and for the wonderful friendships old and new. This book is firmly rooted in the practices of the Art of Hosting.

For my talented dear friend and colleague Mel Geltch, who drew the Design for Wiser Action Canvas: I am so happy that we are in this work together!

For the warm, sparkly and caring Mansi Jasuja, for giving me the title of this book: I am so thankful that we met and look forward to some good co-creative work together.

For my Author Incubator coach, the amazing Angela Lauria: without your amazing program, that makes dreams come true, I would probably still be thinking "maybe I will write a book one day…" thank you for holding space for my dreams and my books.

For my editor, Moriah Howell: I cannot express the debt of gratitude for supporting me through every step of the way, encouraging me and believing in my book, even when I could not see the next step.

To the Morgan James Publishing team: Special thanks to David Hancock, CEO & Founder for believing in me and my message. To my Author Relations Manager, Margo Toulouse, thanks for making the process seamless and easy. Many more thanks to everyone else, but especially Jim Howard, Bethany Marshall, and Nickcole Watkins.

And a big thank you for my family, for Guido and David, for giving me the space and the time to write, in weekends, and evenings in a busy time of transition for our family.

Thank You!

Thanks so much for reading my book!

I hope you got some good ideas and tools to use, to make the change you want in your organization. But, as I have said before, this is no spectator sport… you can make a huge difference, only if you decide to go for it, to take action.

Going down this path is not always easy (especially starting it!): I fully appreciate it. But I hope that you will chose to do it, to go for your ideas and dreams, and bring your ideas, color and beauty to work…because work IS life, not some sad, separate universe.

And you are not alone: there is support for you. DO reach out! (for questions, for stories, for resources).

You can easily contact me through my website of this book: www.playthesystembook.com. I look forward hearing your questions and success stories.

About the Author

Dr. Nora Ganescu is an author, coach, consultant, and trainer.

Her work is helping people bring the best of themselves, achieve their goals and collaborate at work.

Nora started her professional journey twenty-five years ago as a youth activist for intercultural understanding in post-communist Romania, and she has been dedicated to building bridges between people ever since. She went on to work with thousands of employees and executives in companies, NGOs, public administration and international organizations, as an external and internal consultant in over thirty countries and across three continents (Lufthansa, Habitat for Humanity, European Commission and the National Academy for Public Administration are but a few examples).

Nora is a passionate learner, always exploring the frontier of her discipline to bring her clients the best combination of time-tested wisdom and cutting-edge thinking. In her work she combines personal development tools, spiritual nourishment from ancient wisdom schools and insights gleaned from some of the most forward looking and successful companies in the world.

Nora's clients are professionals in every position, who are ready to step up and make a difference that can impact the company and everybody around them.

Nora loves to spend time with her family, read, travel, and being in good conversation.

Printed in the USA
CPSIA information can be obtained
at www.ICGtesting.com
JSHW082357140824
68134JS00020B/2125